SERIES OF SELF-REFLECTIVE STUDIES OF THE WORKS
OF ALLAN KARDEC AND THE GOSPEL OF JESUS

The meaning of the
Divine
Laws
in our lives

This work is an English translation of the original title in Portuguese

O SIGNIFICADO DAS LEIS DIVINAS EM NOSSAS VIDAS©

Translation
Danusa Rangel

Translation Revision
Katie Anderson
Mauricio Cisneiros Filho

Editing
Marcela Santos
Robert Blakely

Graphic designer
Gerson Reis

EDITORA
ESPIRITIZAR

Copyright © 2016 – Editora Espiritizar – Cuiabá, Brazil
(Under partnership with Federação Espirita do Mato Grosso – FEEMT)

ISBN: 978-85-65109-75-8

The meaning of the
Divine
Laws
in our lives

Table of Contents

Introduction

In the book *The Spiritist Center and the Promotion of the Immortal Spirit*, we presented an educational proposal for the human being as a whole, by creating groups of systematic-reflective studies of the works of Allan Kardec in unison with the Gospel of Jesus[1], centered on the Divine Laws and the development of the immortal Spirit's virtues, in a way that we can deepen our understanding of the basic principles of Spiritism, thus fostering our moral transformation, which is the primordial objective of Spiritist postulates.

This modality of study is different from the usual schooling format in that it occurs by creating *Groups of Fraternal Living for the Integral Education of the Being*, in which self-reflective and experience based studies are carried out, focusing on the development of virtues, and basing this development on the teachings of Christ.

It's of fundamental importance for us to review the way we conduct our study activities in Spiritist Centers, giving a new meaning to the studies that are merely intellectual, by engaging in reflection on the Spiritist teachings in our lives and feeling them in our hearts, so that, after all, we can transform ourselves into true Christians, practicing the virtues taught by the Master Jesus.

---

1 Author's note: To obtain greater details about the fundaments of this type of study, consult the book, *The Spiritist Center and the Promotion of the Immortal Spirit*, of our authorship.

This book is the second of the series entitled, *Reflective Studies of the Works of Allan Kardec and the Gospel of Jesus*. Here we present the courses of studies divided didactically into modules to be accomplished in the cited *Groups of Fraternal Living for the Education of the Integral Being*. Since each of these studies are self-explanatory, it's also possible to accomplish each of them individually.

These guides are also useful in supporting Spiritist based public presentations, since the speaker can use the Spiritist Reflections contained in this work as a subsidiary for the lectures of specific themes and sub themes elaborated upon here.

Our objective is to map out a guide of studies which we can reflect upon in a systematic manner regarding Spiritist postulates in conjunction with the Gospel of Jesus. This is the reason why we place such emphasis on the Divine Laws and the exercise of virtues, so that the study can make sense in the lives of students.

This book, second module of the series, elaborates on the meaning of the Divine Laws in our lives, offering all the subsidiaries for the development of the self-reflective method by using real life cases as the illustration of its concepts, an idea taken from the answer to question 919 of *The Spirits' Book*, as it elaborates on a practical method of reaching self-awareness.

We wish excellent reflections to all.

Spiritist Federation of Mato Grosso
Cuiabá, Brazil – June 16, 2016.

1st Meeting

Reflecting on the meaning of the Divine Laws in our lives

Objective – To reflect on the meaning of the Divine Laws in our lives, in order to love, respect and experience them.

Initial self-reflection[2] – *Meditating on the meaning of the Divine Laws in our lives*

- Close your eyes and connect with your inner self, in search of feeling as an immortal Spirit, a child of God, created to evolve and achieve plenitude.

- How do you feel?

- Have you surrendered yourself fully to God and His Laws?

---

2 Author's note: If applying these reflections within a group setting, in order to better facilitate the introspection of the participants, the facilitator could slowly read to the group the self-reflective exercises at the beginning and end of each chapter. It would also be preferable to have calming classical music being played on the background during these moments of reflection.

- Let your thoughts and feelings flow, avoiding masks of self-deceit. Be true to yourself, analyzing yourself with authenticity.

- Now open your eyes, returning to a state of awareness. Write down[3] your experience: the feelings you had, the thoughts that came to mind, the sensations that you benefited from.

Observation: It is very common, in an exercise of self-analysis, for us to stifle the truth, thinking of that which we would like to be true instead of reflecting on that which we in fact feel. This is why we highlight a need for authenticity, remembering that our feelings and sensations never fool us when we are true to ourselves.

REFLECTIONS BASED ON SPIRITISM

In each meeting, we transcribe a series of texts for reflections based on Spiritism, extracted from Allan Kardec's Codification and the Gospel of Jesus, in order to facilitate the reflection during the time available for the meeting. We suggest that the student cross-examines the original books during the interval between meetings. For example, students could observe, in *The Spirits' Book*, the questions that come before and after the ones used in the Spiritist summary, in order to become accustomed to the reflection of the conjunction of books. This will facilitate the understanding of the reason that a certain text was used in the summary and others were not.

---

3 Author's note: Throughout the whole reflective-systemic and systematized study, we suggest some reflections at the beginning and end of the meetings. These reflections are to be accomplished within a designated period of introspection. This is why the students should write down their reflections at the beginning and analyze them at the end of the meeting. Taking notes of the result of these exercises is important for the evaluation of their own development throughout the modules.

QUESTIONS FOR SELF-REFLECTION

At the beginning of each Spiritist self-reflection, we have elaborated questions to help in the reflection on the content studied. They are answered throughout the texts and have the objective of guiding the student to construct or maintain a proactive posture throughout the study. Students are also motivated to become responsible for deciphering themselves the reason behind certain things, and to reflect upon the implications of this knowledge and how it can be applied in their lives, working to feel and experience what they have attained and learned. With this exercise, the purely intellectual study of Spiritism is avoided.

- What is the existential purpose of the immortal Spirit, the mission that it brings in its conscience?

- What is the meaning of the Divine Laws in our lives?

- In regards to human beings, why and for what purpose do these Laws exist?

The mission of the immortal spirit

To understand, in depth, the mission of the immortal Spirit, it's essential that we reflect on question 115 of *The Spirits' Book*, one of the branch-questions[4] of the book:

Question 115. *Are some spirits created good and others bad?*
"God creates all spirits in a state of simplicity and unawareness –

---

4 Author's note: The Spirits' Book has a series of questions that we denominated as branch-questions, since they constitute as a type of key for the understanding of the whole work, such as numbers 115, 614, 621, 625, 632, 642, amongst others. This is why, in the self-reflective study, these questions are systematically repeated, studied and re-studied, exploring different angulations and deepening of the concepts.

that is, without knowledge. To each one God gives a mission: self-enlightenment and gradual achievement of perfection through the pursuit of knowledge and truth. In this way, God draws them ever nearer to the Divine presence. This perfection is, for them, a condition of pure and eternal happiness. Spirits acquire knowledge by passing through trials. Some accept these trials with submission and achieve their goal sooner; others complain and consequently remain distanced from the perfection and happiness promised to them."

Mission of the immortal Spirit: to fulfill the existential purpose of becoming closer to God by attaining knowledge of the Truth and, with this attainment, reaching pure and eternal happiness.

What is the profound, conscientious meaning of the word submission?

Submission: When the immortal Spirit, in tune with its existential purpose, makes efforts to know the Truth and develop virtues, surrendering submissively to the Laws of God, in other words, submitting itself to the conscientious duty of fulfilling the mission that is contained innately within, which is that of reaching relative perfection, possible to all spirits, and gradually becoming closer to the Creator, the Supreme Perfection, when it can be said, as Jesus stated about Himself: *"I am in the Father and the Father is in me"*, then that Spirit will have acquired the right to benefit from the pure and eternal happiness that emanates from the loving omnipresence of God and from within its own being.

What is the profound, conscientious meaning, of the word murmuring?

Murmuring: is the circumstantial process of un-submissive rebelliousness towards the existential purpose, that can last more or less time and have different degrees of manifestation, from the stage of existential emptiness, passing through the existential abandonment, until the stage of existential isolation, to the point of trying to persecute God Himself and, especially others, in the vain attempt to deny the commandments that Jesus taught us. Through this action the Spirit activates the Law of Cause and Effect and, with the lack of submission, creates for itself long periods of pain and suffering, until it humbles its pride, tames its rebelliousness and after having become tired of suffering and wishing to free itself from the weight of suffering, submits itself to the mission of conquering pure and eternal happiness.

This denial of God and of the Divine Laws can be evident or masked. It is evident when the Spirit manifests revolt and rebelliousness in a very clear and evident manner. It is masked when the Spirit rebels in a way that may seem submissive, but since the focus is on seeming and not actually being submissive, the process is false in itself.

What is this truth that we have the mission of knowing in order to become closer to God? This Truth is all the Divine Laws combined; such Laws that we should love and practice in order to develop virtues.

Returning to reflect on *The Spirits' Book*:

Question 614. *What does the term "natural law" mean?*
"The law of nature is the law of God. It is the only rule that ensures human happiness, since it reveals what you as human beings should and should not do, and since you only suffer when you disobey it."

Question 616. *Can God have given us laws in one era and then revoked them in another?*
"God cannot be mistaken. Humanity has to change its laws periodically because the latter are flawed. But the laws of God are perfect. The harmony that regulates both the material and ethical realms is based on laws established from all Eternity."

Question 619. *Has God given us the means of knowing the law?*
"All of you may know it, but not all of you will understand it. The ones who understand it best are those who seek their inner transformation through love. One day, however, everyone will comprehend it: that is the destiny toward which progress is inevitably leading you."

Question 620. *Does a spirit understand the law of God more clearly before or after an incarnation?*
"Its understanding depends on how evolved it is. After being united with a body, it will preserve an intuitive memory of the law. But it will ignore the law whenever the lower instincts come to dominate its nature."

Question 621. *Where is the law of God written?*
"In the conscience."
a) Since we carry the law of God in our consciences, why was it necessary to reveal it to us?
"You had forgotten or misunderstood it. God then willed that it should be recalled to your memory."

To know the Truth, therefore, is to get into contact, in a conscientious manner, with the Divine Laws that we bring inscribed in our own conscience. Those who submit themselves to the mission that they bring are the ones who strive, in a conscientious manner, to understand these Laws so that they can love and fulfill them; the ones who murmur are the ones who, by cultivating bad instincts, strive to forget and disregard them.

The great objective of Jesus incarnating amongst us was to reveal them; which is the same mission as that of the superior Spirits who brought us Spiritism.

It's up to us, as incarnated Beings to study and reflect upon the Gospel of Jesus, and Kardec's Codification and the supplementary works of Spiritism, in order to investigate how the Laws work, so that we will feel love for the Laws, which were created so that we can be happy when we have fulfilled them.

Next, we will study the evangelical precept: *Know the Truth, and the Truth will set you free*. (John, 8:32), correlated with the question 115 of *The Spirits' Book*.

We see that Jesus did not say that knowledge will set us free, but rather, the Truth. In the precept, we have a triad: knowledge of the Truth, feeling of the Truth and experiencing the Truth. With these steps we overcome the three levels of ignorance: not knowing, not feeling and not experiencing, as can be seen in figure 1:

LIVING

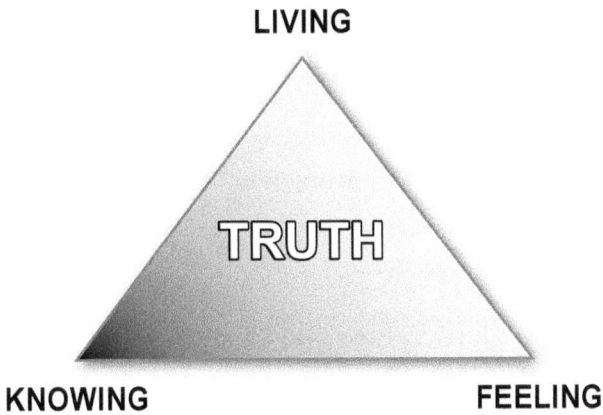

KNOWING　　　　　　**FEELING**

Figure 1 – The Dimensions of the Truth

The whole process of knowing happens first at a reasoning level, because everything starts in the thought, in reason. When Jesus says "Know *the truth*", a hint is given about the Truth that sets us free, that is, the Divine Laws that summarize the Truth in the core of each one of us.

This dimension of the Truth corresponds to loving God with all our *understanding*, that is, the understanding of the meaning of His laws in our lives.

From then on, we will be invited to exercise this truth in order to feel it in our hearts. From the moment in which we become accustomed to reflecting, even if we cannot feel this truth immediately, with the whole vigor of our hearts, it will remain shining in our conscience. This dimension of the Truth corresponds to loving the Laws of God with all our hearts.

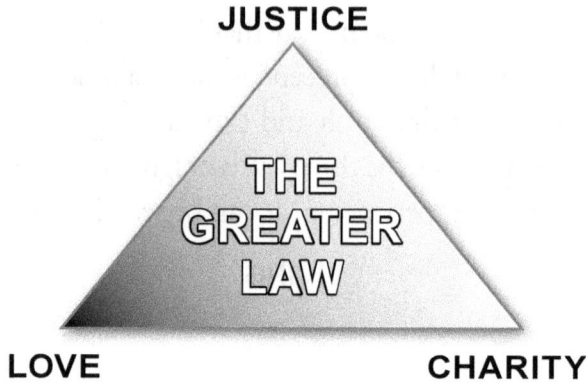

JUSTICE

THE
GREATER
LAW

LOVE   **CHARITY**

Figure 2 – The Dimensions of the Greater Law

The love for the Divine Laws is the path that brings us closer to God, especially the Greater Laws, represented in figure 2, with its three dimensions: Justice, Love and Charity:

Loving the Divine Laws present in our conscience, in order to practice them, is a great act of self-love that causes happiness in the fulfillment of the Law of Justice, since this Law entails that we all have the right to happiness, as can been seen in question 115 of *The Spirits' Book*, studied previously. (God has given each of them a mission. It's aimed at enlightening them and progressively leading them toward perfection through knowledge of the truth in order to draw them nearer to God. In that perfection, they will find **eternal bliss** without any troubles.)

Nevertheless, happiness is more than a right, since no one can benefit from a right without carrying out a duty. The conquest of happiness happens, therefore, through the practice of the dimensions of Love and Charity of the Greater Law, constituting itself in the grand conscientious duty that we are invited to gain.

When we accomplish the movement of loving the Divine

Laws, loving ourselves, we will be practicing the Law of Love. The Law of Charity is practiced by loving one another, doing unto others that which we want them to do to us, learning to pass through the filter of Justice, Love and Charity everything that we do to ourselves and to others.

Therefore, it's only possible to practice the Divine Laws by developing the virtues indicated in each Law. For example, the Law of Love is fulfilled by developing the virtue of love, the Law of Freedom, with the virtue of discernment and so forth.

We observe in figure 3, the illustration of the dimension for the evolution of the being: God, Divine Laws and Self, immortal Spirit. In the process of evolution, the immortal Spirit is invited toward two movements – **surrender and action:** to *surrender* itself lovingly to God and the Divine laws and to *act* developing the essential virtues of Life.

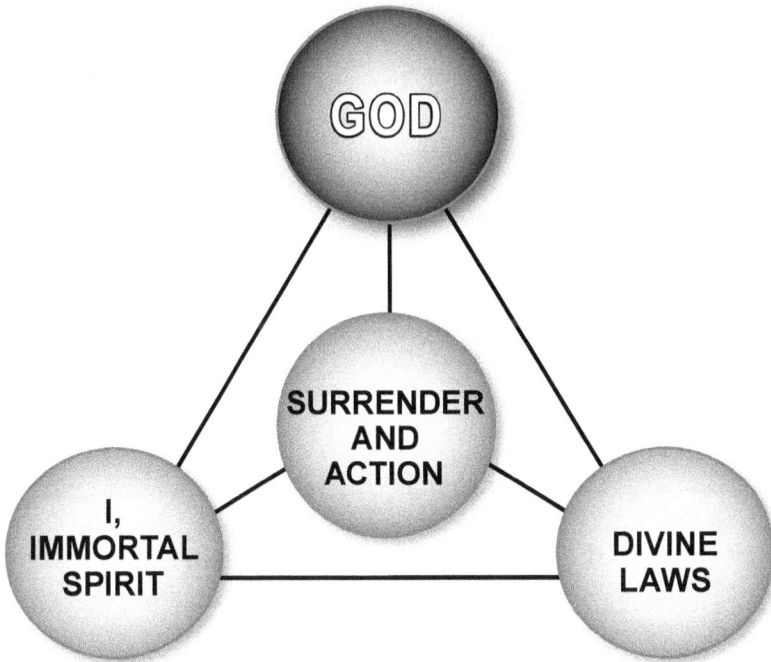

Figure 3 – The Dimensions of the Evolution of the Being

This is the proposal for all of us: to surrender ourselves to God and His Laws, fulfilling His Will, practicing the Greater Law, the Law of Love, Justice and Charity and all the other Laws that are conjugated, acting through the Self, immortal Spirit, the Essential and immortal Being that we are, developing the essential virtues, that correspond to these Laws.

Just like the Divine Laws, virtues already exist in a blatant form in our conscience, and the development is manifested in a practical means of loving and experiencing the Laws of God.

We can compare virtues to the seeds of a great orchid. We bring them to germination and should cultivate them, transforming them into verdurous trees, filled with flavorsome fruits that offer pure and eternal happiness. The process of evolution is the fruit of two forces, **blessing** and **conquest**. The Laws and the seeds of virtues are God's blessings for us to evolve and reach pure and eternal happiness. This happiness is the fruit of the conquest in which we worked to develop through the virtues within us, in tune with the Laws of Labor and of Progress.

So that we can conquer this happiness, consequent to the knowledge of the Truth and of becoming closer to God, we go through trials in various corporeal existences until we complete the purification process.

SELF-REFLECTIVE EVALUATION

- Close your eyes and connect with your inner self, in search of the content studied in this meeting.

- Analyze yourself in an authentic manner, avoiding self-deceit.

- From the content, what did you understand that applies to your life?

- Did the content studied change the way you feel the Divine Laws within yourself? If so, what changes occurred?

- What did you understand about the mission of the immortal Spirit? Did you notice in yourself submission to the Will of God or are you still defying His Will?

- Knowing that un-submissiveness can be evident or masked, does this apply to you? How do you feel the manifestations of your un-submission?

- What do you understand from the three dimensions of the Truth: to know, to feel and to live? What is your perspective?

- What did you understand about the three dimensions of the Greater Law: Justice, Love and Charity? What perspectives are opening to you as a result of this understanding?

- What do you understand from the three dimensions of evolution of the immortal Spirit: Self, Immortal Spirit, Divine Laws and God? You are being invited to surrender to God and to His Laws and act towards developing virtues in yourself. What perspective has opened to you before this understanding?

- What is it like for you to feel God before these triads: the three dimensions of Truth, the three dimensions of the Greater Law and the three dimensions of evolution of the immortal Spirit?

- So that the triad can be effective in your life, it's essential to develop these three virtues: Justice, Love and Charity. How do you feel making efforts to develop them? Do you feel it's possible for you to make it a common exercise in your life or is there still some resistance to this practice? Analyze yourself in an authentic manner, avoiding self-deceit[5].

- How do you feel when applying the content studied in your life? Do you feel that it can improve your life as you search for self-transformation in the practice of good deeds?

- Now, recognize yourself as the immortal Spirit you are, who brings within the divine purview the determination to evolve until reaching relative perfection, through the pure understanding of the fulfilment of the Divine Laws, through the practice of virtues and through the search of unity, by striving to be one with God. Submerge yourself profoundly into this spiritual truth. Feel and see yourself fulfilling the Divine Laws and developing all the essential virtues of Life throughout time, feeling the loving presence of God in your life.

- Gradually, start returning to a state of awareness. Open your eyes and write down your reflections.

---

5 Authors note: When an objection exists within us, we can feel some resistance that is manifested as a disconnection and a sensation of discomfort when we formulate the question internally. This means a need to work on the questions. If this takes place, it is imperative to remain confident that all and every limitation is possible to be transmuted through time throughout continuous effort, patiently and perseveringly.

2nd Meeting

Applying the Divine Laws in professional relationships

part I

Objective – To reflect on the meaning of the Divine Laws in our lives, in order to love, respect and apply them in our professional relationships.

Initial reflection – *Meditating on the meaning of the Divine Laws in our lives.*

- Close your eyes and connect with your inner self, in search of feeling as an immortal Spirit, a child of God, created to evolve and achieve plenitude.
- How do you feel?
- Have you surrendered yourself fully to God and His Laws?

- How have you dealt with the Divine Laws in your professional activities? Have you been applying them?

- Let your thoughts and feelings flow, avoiding any masks, or self-deceit. Be true to yourself, analyzing yourself with authenticity.

- Now open your eyes, returning to a state of awareness. Write down your experience: the feelings you had, the thoughts that came to mind, the sensations that you benefited from.

REFLECTIONS BASED ON SPIRITISM
QUESTIONS FOR SELF-REFLECTION

- Knowing that the Divine Laws are present in our conscience and that they exist for us to reach pure and eternal happiness, what actions can be accomplished to love and fulfill them in our professional activities?

- What are the practical means that can be used to develop virtues, fulfilling the Divine Laws?

The exercise of doing good deeds with an existential purpose

In our previous meeting we learned that we are invited to exercise the Divine Laws, developing the essential virtues, behaving submissively towards the goals that exist within our conscience so that we may become closer to God through the knowledge of the Truth, manifesting His attributes in ourselves.

In this meeting, we will continue to reflect on the meaning of the Divine Laws in our lives, reflecting on the distinction between what is truly good, which is acting in accordance with the Laws of God and the evil that it is to trespass them.

We will also see a practical method of reflecting on the Laws in order to use them in all our daily activities.

Let's take a look at some questions in *The Spirits' Book*, relating to the Divine Laws that we are conscientiously invited to utilize, pointing our free will towards the paths of goodness.

Question 629. *How would you define the ethical law?*
"The ethical law is the rule for proper action, that is to say, for distinguishing practically between the good and the bad. It is founded on the observance of the law of God. You act rightly when you take the good of everyone as your aim and rule for action. To the extent that you do so, you obey the law of God."

Question 630. *How can we distinguish between good and bad?*
"Good is anything that conforms to the law of God; bad is anything that departs from it. To do right is to conform to the law of God; to do wrong is to break it."

Question 631. *Do we have it in our power to distinguish between good and bad?*
"Yes, you do when you believe in God and desire to do what is right. God has given you intelligence in order to discriminate between the two."

Question 632. *Since we are subject to error, can't we be mistaken in our appreciation of good and bad and believe that we are doing right when, in fact, we are doing wrong?*
"Jesus has said: 'So always treat others as you would like them to treat you.' The whole of the ethical law is contained in that commandment. Make it your rule of action, and you will never go wrong."

Question 642. *In insuring our future happiness, is it enough simply not to have done anything wrong?*
"No. You must do good, and to the utmost of your ability. Each

of you is responsible, both for all the wrong you have done and all the good you have failed to do."

We can see that the parameters to practice goodness are very clear in these answers. When we truly want to practice it, we use our intelligence to distinguish what is in accordance with the Divine Laws, especially the Greater Law, studied in the previous meeting, being loveable and fair, doing unto others that which we would like them to do to us.

The parameter is always the Greater Law and the development of the virtues of love, justice and charity.

Although the standards are very clear, can we fool ourselves into believing that we are doing good, when in truth we are doing something wrong? Yes, through the process of conscious or subconscious self-deceit.

To better understand self-deceit, we will study the message "Duty", from the Spirit Lazarus, published in *The Gospel According to Spiritism*, chapter XVII, item 7:

"Duty is a moral obligation, first to the self and then to others. Duty is a fundamental law of life. It is expressed in the smallest and in the most elevated human actions. I speak here, you must understand, only of moral duty – rather than the obligations owed, for instance, to your profession.

Duty is one of the most difficult attributes to act on because it is often in conflict with personal interests and desires of the heart. Its victories have no witnesses; its defeats go unnoticed. As such, duty is, in essence, a matter of free will. The conscience acts as the guardian of virtue as well as its caretaker, but frequently it is powerless against the deceptions of desire.

Duty, if you attend to it faithfully, lifts you up spiritually. But, you will ask, is it possible to define duty with any precision? Where does duty begin? Where does it end? I will say that your duty begins precisely at the point where the peace and happiness of your neighbor is threatened by your actions; it ends at that point beyond which you wouldn't like anyone to cross, with respect to yourself.

God has created everyone equal where suffering is concerned. Tall and short, ignorant and educated alike, suffer for identical reasons, i.e., to understand the depth of pain human actions can cause. The same is not true of goodness, whose expressions are more varied and complex. Do understand that equality in the face of pain is part of the Divine Plan. God wants everyone, informed by experience, to stop doing wrong and hiding behind excuses of not knowing its consequences.

Duty is a practical expression of all moral theories. It is the bravery of the soul that withstands the struggles of life. Duty is both austere and resilient, adaptable to the knottiest complexities and yet inflexible before temptation. Those who fulfill their duty show that they love God above all things, and their fellow human beings more than themselves. Duty is simultaneously judge and slave of its own cause.

Duty is the most beautiful laurel in the grove of reason. Reason nurtures the sense of duty, much as a mother nurses her child. You should love duty not because it spares you from the wrongs of life – no one escapes those – but because it gives your soul vigor, which it needs in order to grow.

The sense of duty grows and shines forth in increasingly more elevated forms as humanity progresses. Your obligation toward God has no end. You must ultimately express in yourself the most sublime virtues, for this is the aim of God, Who will not settle for an unfinished picture. God expects all the beauty of your soul to shine in all its grandeur. – Lazarus (Paris, 1863).

Lazarus elaborates on two questions: The Law of Duty and the virtue of duty. The Law is the sting of the conscience, so that we can, through the means of this guardian of inner rectitude, develop the attributes of the Creator in ourselves, reflecting the virtues of the Eternal, reaching relative perfection.

We therefore, have the conscientious duty of manifesting the divine attributes, drawing ever nearer to God, and fulfilling the mission for which we were destined.

Therefore, as the spiritual Benefactor has said, although duty is the sting of conscience – *the guardian of inner rectitude – which warns and upholds the sense of duty, but it is held back, often powerless before the **sophistry** of passion.*

Let's reflect on the concept of sophism according to the Houaiss dictionary: argument or rationale conceived with the objective of producing an illusion of the truth, that, although it stimulates concord with the rules of reason, presents in reality, an internal structure, which is inconsistent, incorrect and deliberately deceiving.

Psychologically, the **sophisms of passion** are false behaviors in which the person sought, consciously or unconsciously, to develop pseudo-goodness. When the action is conscious, the person acts in bad faith, in order to deceive others. When it's unconscious, the person believes him or herself to be proceeding well, when in truth, is following a path of pseudo-goodness, which is much easier than achieving actual goodness, since that would depend on continued, patient, perseverant and disciplined efforts to develop the essential virtues of Life, to love and fulfill the Divine Laws, manifesting the divine attributes[6] in oneself, as we can see in figure 4.

---

6 Author's note: In order to know in more detail about the divine attributes, we suggest to the reader the book The Loving Presence of God In Our Lives, of our authorship, Editor Espiritizar, the first book of this series.

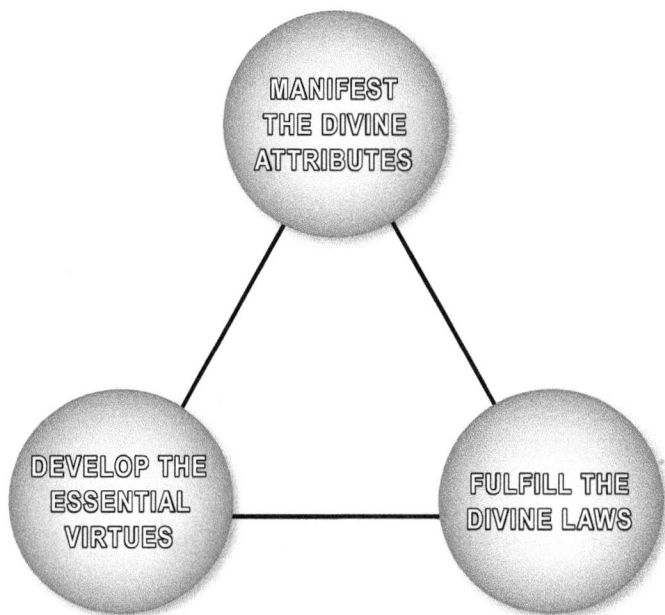

Figure 4 – The Conditions for Developing Goodness

Therefore, we are invited to practice the Divine Laws through the development of the essential virtues, acting submissively to the method that we bring in our conscience so that we can become closer to God through the understanding of the Truth, manifesting His attributes in us.

We will study various cases in this module of Reflective Studies, of the Works of Allan Kardec and the Gospel of Jesus, using the perspective that Allan Kardec defines in question 919 of *The Spirits' Book*: *"In the present life, how can we guarantee our own ethical progress and our ability to resist our lower tendencies? One of your wise men has told you, 'Know thyself.'"*

When we study a content and at the same time apply it in our lives, the learning becomes effective, because we are not simply guiding ourselves with theoretical concepts, but we are also internalizing the Christian Spiritist postulates, thus generating in us self-transformation.

To establish the practical means that St. Augustine refers to in questions 919 and 919a we use a few didactic resources. Firstly, by analyzing the cases, starting from the Divine Laws that are disrespected through ego-based behavior. Next, by analyzing the divine attributes that are exercised, and last, by analyzing how a person can act in order to develop virtues that will transmute ego-based vices, lovingly fulfilling the Laws and manifesting the attributes of God within, in the perspective studied in Module 1 of these series, in the book *The Loving Presence of God in our Lives*, also published by – Editora Espiritizar.

All of the cases that we study are based on true facts, so that the study can be as pragmatic as possible. We have modified the names of the persons involved in order to keep their identities private.

When studying a case, it is important that we do not judge someone else's behaviors. The objective of studying real cases is to reflect upon the mistakes of others so that we may learn in order for us not to commit the same errors. This is why, it's necessary to make reflections a habit in our lives, each of us asking of ourselves: if this had happened to me, would I have acted in a different way or would I have acted in the same way or in an even more unbalanced manner than the protagonist of the study?

In this meeting we will study the case of a professor named Joseph, to exemplify a very common question of the professional relationships: **of personal responsibility.**

Joseph is a professor at a university where he teaches in the health department and shares its responsibilities with a colleague who acts in a negligent manner, not fulfilling the tasks that are entrusted to him, in detriment to the students.

The students often relate to Joseph the difficult experiences they've had with the other professor and Joseph gets very angry. He feels plenty of rage and mad about his colleague's negligence, but does not say anything in order to avoid getting into a quarrel with him.

His anger towards his colleagues' posture is so great that he reaches the point of developing physical problems, a duodenal ulcer and psoriasis, also emotional issues, such as the disorder of generalized anxiety, all due to this tumultuous relationship with his colleague. He feels frustrated about not being able to do anything to correct the situation.

Since he's worried about the future of his students, he thinks, often times, about calling out his colleague to say how very irresponsible he is and that his actions are not dignified, but instead, Joseph remains inactive and angry.

As he does nothing to help resolve the problem, Joseph lives day in and day out saying to himself: *I should do something to resolve this. I cannot leave things this way…* he laments but remains inactive.

The students, in turn, besides expressing their disgust with the mistaken posture of the negligent professor, also do not do anything and only relate to Professor Joseph what is taking place, asking him to take action directly against his colleague, or indirectly by talking to the university's coordinating body.

* * *

Let's analyze the case of Joseph under the light of the triad: Immortal Spirit, Divine Laws and God, in which he is invited to develop the essential virtues, fulfilling the Divine Laws and manifesting the divine attributes.

Initially, we will reflect on which Divine Laws Joseph is refusing to fulfill. In the case of interpersonal relationships, the main Divine Law to guide him is the **Law of Freedom**. By becoming indisposed with his colleague because of the way he acts, Joseph wants to confront the freewill of others.

He wants to solve his colleague's negligence problem and at the same time the problem of his students who remain in a comfort zone waiting for his reaction.

He confronts the **Law of Free Will**, and at the same time does not observe various other Laws as well, such as the Law **of Solidarity, of Responsibility**, and mainly the **Law of Love, Justice and Charity.**

Let's reflect: Joseph's actions are not solidary, neither to his colleague, nor to his students, let alone to himself. His actions are also pseudo-responsible, since he gives the impression that he is very responsible, but acts irresponsibly in a different way, he acts irresponsibly when he does not do anything to help to resolve the problem.

Joseph's actions are, above all, unloving, unjust and uncharitable. Let's take a look: is he being loving, just and charitable to himself? No! He's not fulfilling the Law of Love Justice and Charity, starting with himself, by creating afflictions for himself as he starts revolting against the freewill of others. This is why Joseph is physically and emotionally ill. These are the actual causes of his afflictions, created by not fulfilling the Divine Laws.

In *The Gospel according to Spiritism*, Allan Kardec studies this matter. Let's read chapter V items 4 and 5 – *Current causes of afflictions*, from which we have reproduced a few extracts:

[...]

We ask each of you who has experienced heartaches because of disappointments and losses to study your own consciences closely, going back, step by step, to the origins of each problem that is causing you pain. More likely than not, most will be able to say: If I had done, or not done, such and such a thing, I wouldn't be where I am today.

Who is, in such cases, responsible for the sufferings if not the person who suffers? In most cases, men and women are the architects of their own troubles. Yet rather than admit this fact, they usually find it easier and less humiliating to their egos to blame their troubles on fate, God, bad luck, or even on an unlucky star. However, this "unlucky star" is actually no more than their own carelessness. [...]

However, God, Who desires the progress of every soul, doesn't allow detours from the upright path to go unnoticed. There is no wrong, no infraction of the Divine Law, however small, that doesn't carry its own consequences. In small things, as in great, people are always corrected according to their wrongs. The suffering that follows is always a warning. Through it, we humans gain valuable knowledge that allows us to distinguish between right and wrong. Thus we realize the necessity of bettering ourselves so that in the future we can avoid the behavior whose negative consequences we now feel. Without such consequences, progress would be slower and human beings would be even farther from our blissful destination.

If we do not fulfill the Law of Love Justice and Charity towards ourselves, it will be impossible to fulfill them in relation to others. That is why we immerse ourselves more and more into evil. There is no way of giving to others that which we do not have within ourselves. When this happens, we activate other Divine Laws, such as of **Cause and Effect** which will make the consequences of our errors return to us.

That is what happened to Joseph, when he didn't fulfill the Divine Laws. He became ill, developing physical and emotional problems that are the consequences of his actions. These consequences *gave him valuable knowledge allowing him to distinguish between right and wrong.*

As we reflect upon the text of Allan Kardec, regarding the current causes of afflictions, it becomes clear that the Law of Cause and Effect is not a Law of punishment, but rather, exists to protect us from ourselves, since when we feel physical or moral pain, resulting from our failure in fulfilling the Divine Laws, we are invited to change our conduct to avoid the indefinite halt upon our happiness.

Other Laws that Joseph confronts are the Laws of **Duty and of Evolution**. He does not fulfill his own duty, wanting to be the guardian of someone else's conscience, as if this were possible. That is why he does not fulfill the Law of Freedom.

It's important to remember that the Divine Laws are solidary to one another and that, by confronting one, all the remaining are, in greater or lesser intensity unfulfilled. As we cannot study in such a short space of time all the Laws, we are only didactically studying the main laws that are usually confronted.

SELF-REFLECTIVE EVALUATION

- Close your eyes and connect with your inner self, exploring the content studied in this meeting.

- Analyze yourself in an authentic manner, avoiding self-deceit.

- From the content studied, what did you understand that applies to your life?

- Did this study change the way you feel the Divine Laws in yourself? If so, what are the changes?

- What did you understand in relation to the practice of goodness as a process of loving and fulfilling the Divine Laws?

- In this meeting, we reflected on the concept of submission towards God through the exercise of conscientious duty, and also discussed murmuring as an un-submissive rebellion. Feel within yourself the conscientious duty of fulfilling the existential purpose of becoming closer to God. What did you understand about the guardian duty of inner rectitude of the immortal Spirit? Did you notice yourself in tune with the Law of Duty? How do you feel?

• Reflect also on the importance of making efforts to develop the conscientious duty of acting upon the attributes of God in our lives, submitting to His Laws. Search your feelings to find this possibility within yourself. How do you feel it? How does it feel to make these efforts?

• Proceeding from a more profound understanding of the Divine Laws, in your life, and the development of the essential virtues as an example of the practice of these Laws, has there been an amplification of the desire to develop these virtues? How does it feel?

• How do you feel about making efforts to love and exercise the Divine Laws, accomplishing goodness to the limit of your strength? Do you feel it's possible for you to make this a usual practice in your life or is there still some resistance to this exercise?

• How do you feel about applying the content studied in your life? Do you feel that it can improve your life in the search of self-transformation and in the acts of good deeds?

• Now, recognize yourself as the immortal Spirit you are, who brings within the divine purview the determination to evolve until reaching relative perfection, through the pure understanding of the fulfilment of the Divine Laws, through the practice of virtues and through the search of unity, by striving to be one with God. Submerge yourself profoundly into this spiritual truth. Feel and see yourself fulfilling the Divine Laws and developing all the essential virtues of Life throughout time, feeling the loving presence of God in your life.

• Gradually, start returning to a state of alertness. Open your eyes and write down your reflections.

34 | THE MEANING OF THE DIVINE LAWS IN OUR LIVES

3rd Meeting

Applying the Divine Laws in professional relationships

part II

Objective – To reflect on the meaning of the Divine Laws in our lives, in order to love, respect, and apply them in our professional relationships.

Initial reflection – *Meditating on the meaning of the Divine Laws in our lives.*

- Close your eyes and connect with your inner self, in search of feeling as an immortal Spirit, a child of God, created to evolve and achieve plenitude.

- How do you feel?

- Have you surrendered yourself fully to God and His Laws?

- How have you dealt with the Divine Laws in your professional activities? Have you been applying them?

- Let your thoughts and feelings flow, avoiding any masks of self-deceit. Be true to yourself, analyzing yourself with authenticity.

- Now open your eyes, returning to a state of awareness. Write down your experience: the feelings you had, the thoughts that came to mind, the sensations that you benefited from.

REFLECTIONS BASED ON SPIRITISM
QUESTIONS FOR SELF-REFLECTION

- Knowing that the Divine Laws are present in our conscience and that they exist for us to reach pure and eternal happiness, what actions can we take in order to love and fulfill them in our professional activities?

- What practical means can we use to manifest the divine attributes and develop the essential virtues of Life?

In our last meeting we initiated a study on the case of Professor Joseph, reviewing his attitudes that prevented him from fulfilling the Divine Laws. In this meeting we will continue to study this case, looking at the divine attributes that he didn't fulfill and what can be done in order to fulfill the Laws, manifest the attributes, and to develop the essential virtues of Life.

Consequences of distancing oneself from the divine attributes

We will go a little deeper into our reflections, analyzing the divine attributes, so that we can dive into other nuances of the case of Professor Joseph [7], thus increasing our understanding of his lack of fulfillment of the Laws.

Next, we will present – *The Loving Presence of God in Our Lives* – in a summarized manner, as a review of the divine attributes studied in that book.

Oneness

Submission – *individualization* – process in which a person becomes more and more humanized, to the point of being able to initiate the ascension towards angelic enlightenment.

Evident murmuring – *dehumanization* – process of hardening the human being through the exacerbation of the passions.

Masked murmuring – *personalist* – a process that causes all other behaviors of deceitfulness of being, creating a persona similar to the Pharisees from the time of Jesus.

Supreme Goodness and Justice

Submission – **goodness and justice** – the virtues of goodness and justice are produced by the action of the Spirit submitting to its mission of knowing, loving, respecting and living the Divine Laws present in its own conscience, thus gaining proximity to God through the cultivation of the essential virtues.

---

7 Author's note: We suggest that before proceeding, you read the case found in the previous chapter.

Evident murmuring – evilness and injustice – the Spirit enters into a process of dehumanization that is produced by a revolt against the Divine Laws. This revolt is the cause of evil, injustice and cruelty.

Masked murmuring – pseudo-goodness and pseudo-justice – a process in which the Spirit becomes a personalist and fakes its submission to the Divine Laws, making it look like it is good and just while in reality it is only covering up the evilness, injustice and cruelty that it commits.

Immateriality

Submission – *spirituality and dematerialization* – a process in which the Spirit, by means of individualization becomes more and more virtuous, or even, self-enlightens, working towards its own dematerialization, purifying itself until angelic enlightenment.

Evident murmuring – *materialism* – a process caused by dehumanization, resulting from the cultivation of material things that causes the hardening of a human being through the exacerbation of the passions.

Masked murmuring – *pseudo-spiritualization* – a process caused by personalism, in which the person becomes a spiritualist-materialist, appearing to cultivate spiritualization, but in truth, behaving materialistically, as the Pharisees did during Jesus's times.

Immutability

Submission – *essential immutability* – the condition of the children of God created for relative perfection and to benefit from pure and eternal happiness is essentially immutable. In this resides a divine determination which no being has the power of impeding. If it were any different God would not be omnipotent.

Evident murmuring – *volubility* – resulting from materialism, which makes the person enter into a process of superficiality in life.

Masked murmuring – *pseudo-inalterability* – a process also cause by personalism, in which the person crystallizes their masked postures, seemingly unchangeable, crystallized through the passions produced through limited beliefs, focused on "seeming", to the detriment of "being", resulting in a distancing from God and happiness.

Eternity

Submission – *immortality with occupation in the eternal present* – as the immortal Spirits that we are, with a beginning and no end, we become eternal from the moment in which we are created. When the Spirit **occupies itself** with the present, it can feel its immortality and eternity, its consequent destination and its pure and eternal happiness. For this reason it evolves free of any conflict.

Evident murmuring – *pos-occupation* – process in which the Spirit fixates on lamentation in relation to the past, about what it did or did not do, becoming very conflicted.

Masked murmuring – *pre-occupation* – process in which the Spirit fixates on the future and becomes anxious about *what will be*, creating unnecessary conflicts, since it wishes to control the future, when such control belongs only to God.

Omnipotence

Submission – *potency* – using the power that we have innately in ourselves, the one that accomplished the transformation in our own lives, searching for our individuality through the practice of virtues, manifesting the divine attributes within ourselves, becoming a live potential of the Universe, fulfilling the supreme will of God.

Evident murmuring – *impotence* – process in which the Spirit enters into a state of inertia, becoming involved in its own mental inertia, not wishing to submit to the Laws of Labor and Progress, believing it does not have the strength to evolve through its own efforts.

Masked murmuring – *pseudo – omnipotence and despotism* – process in which the Spirit attempts, in vain, to compete with God, in the belief that it is in possession of having a super power, thus supposing it is capable of everything and, for this reason, attempts to impose its despotism upon itself and others around it.

Omniscience

Submission – *conscience* – resulting from harmonization with the mission of the immortal Spirit, that is, to know the Truth in order to approach God.

Evident murmuring – *unconscious* – resulting from actions contrary to the immortal Spirit, which lets itself be seduced by egocentric and individualistic materialism, becoming reckless.

Masked murmuring – *pseudo-conscience* – process produced through personalism, by the Spirit that believes it possesses knowledge that in reality it does not have, culminating in actions that are pseudo-omnipotent and despotic in competition with God.

Omnipresence

Submission – *presence* – when the Spirit decides to submit to the Divine Laws, and starts feeling the presence of God in its own Essence through the effort of reaching for the Truth, building the Kingdom of God in itself.

Evident murmuring – *annulment* – a process caused by an unawareness in relation to Life, resulting in dehumanization, which is due to inconsequence, and causes the Spirit to strive uselessly to annul itself, in a vain attempt to run from the presence of God within itself.

Masked murmuring – *isolation* – a process caused by personalism, in which the Spirit, believing to be wise, isolates itself unilaterally from God and from its own essence. This causes a great sense of inner emptiness.

The greatest limitation that Professor Joseph vitalizes is **personalism**. Since he assumes the characteristic of the '**good guy**', believing that he should always please everyone.

We can see the characteristics of personalism in Joseph's story: **Joseph becomes embittered with the situation of the students**; He feels anger towards his colleague, whose negligence he sees as a dereliction of duty, **but does not say anything, in order to avoid a dispute**; He feels frustrated by **not being able to do anything**; He often thinks about calling his colleague to tell him that he is irresponsible and that his actions are undignified, **but he remains inactive, stymied by his inner revolt.**

As personalism is the foundation of ego-based sentiments that distances us from the attribute of God, other problems emerge, such as **pseudo-kindness** and **pseudo-justice**, attitudes that are derived from personalism. We notice that Professor Joseph's kindness is false, because even though his intention is positive in wanting to help the students, the direction in which this intention has taken him is completely wrong, because he acts in a cruel and unjust manner toward himself and his colleague, as well as with pseudo-kindness and pseudo-justice toward his students, feeling sorry for them, but not taking any positive actions. These last two characteristics also manifest with the colleague, since Joseph does not say anything in order not to upset himself.

Another ego-based sentiment which is vitalized by Joseph is connivance which appears to take place toward the students as much as toward his colleague. The students themselves do not do anything to change the situation and have a false feeling of solidarity toward Professor Joseph as they wait for him to resolve their problems. Professor Joseph, acts as a "good colleague", toward the negligent professor, out of a desire to be on "good" terms with others. Within this posture, he is also turning a blind eye to his own interior feelings, but he remains nevertheless, angry.

Why is he cruel and unfair to himself and to his colleague? We see in the story: **He feels plenty of rage toward his colleague, and revulsion for his negligence**, but does not say anything in order to avoid a dispute. His reaction towards his colleague's posture is so great that he begins developing physical problems, a **duodenal ulcer and psoriasis**, as well as emotional issues, such as a **disorder of generalized anxiety**, resulting directly from the troublesome relationship he maintains with his colleague; he often thinks about **calling his colleague to tell him that he is very irresponsible and that his actions are not dignified.**

The revulsion and anger maintained by Joseph, is not only harmful for him, but his energy will certainly reach his colleague through hateful vibrations. This is why his posture is characterized as an oscillating movement of a pendulum, which balances between, **personalism** and **dehumanization; pseudo-kindness** and **pseudo justice** and **cruelty** and **unfairness.**

To escape this **volubility**, Joseph enters into a movement of **pseudo-inalterability**, since he spends the whole time *seeming*, to

42 | THE MEANING OF THE DIVINE LAWS IN OUR LIVES

the detriment of *being*. This happens to every person that develops a persona. The mask that they vitalize only hides the ego-based feelings, which distances them from the attributes of God, disturbing them internally, while externally maintaining masks of excellent people.

In relation to the attribute of eternity, Professor Joseph does not **concern** himself with the problem that needs to be resolved, but gives into the masked murmuring of **preoccupation** and the evident posture of **post-occupation**. He is concerned with the future of the students who will be poorly educated by the other professor and also by the negligence of his colleague, but he continues immobile, only lamenting that he does not do anything to resolve the problem.

There are two unsolvable questions that are a source of preoccupation for the immortal Spirit: the future and the changes of external circumstances. Professor Joseph wants to change the future and his colleague. With this attitude, besides distancing himself from occupation with the present time, which is the correct manner of dealing with time, he tries to disrespect the **Law of Freedom**, as we have previously studied. By trying to interfere in the freewill of his colleague, Joseph creates an unsolvable problem for himself, by consequently unbalancing himself emotionally.

When post-occupying (concerning himself only about the future), lamenting his attitude, Professor Joseph doesn't do anything to change the problem. The only positive thing that can be done with our mistakes is to learn from them in order to repair whatever damage they might have caused; Joseph never takes these steps and only concentrates his attention on lamenting over his own mistakes.

In order for us to manifest the divine attributes in ourselves, loving and respecting the Divine Laws, we must center ourselves and reframe or assign a new meaning to our own values. Many people may question: But should I let the other do what they want? This is not the meaning of respecting the Law of Free will. We will return to this question later.

We will continue reflecting on the divine attributes that Joseph refuses to develop, believing that he is acting correctly.

In relation to the attribute of **divine omnipotence**, Professor Joseph oscillates between **pseudo- omnipotence/despotism** and **impotence**. To understand the distancing of this attribute it's necessary to reflect on two concepts: **existential and circumstantial.**

Existential – everything to do with the existence of the immortal Spirit, its evolution by means of its moral transformation, developing the essential virtues of Life, fulfilling the Divine Laws and manifesting the divine attributes within. These are the values pertinent to the Existential Being, fulfilling its inner world, in an individual and nontransferable manner.

Circumstantial – everything regarding the various activities related to the external world. They are transitory and mutable, depending on the moment lived by the Being. They are essential to acquiring the specific essential virtues of Life that are necessary for this level of existential evolution.

Whenever the Spirit enters into sync with the existential matters of life, he fulfills the Divine Laws, developing virtues, conducting various circumstantial activities in a natural and balanced process. On the other hand, whenever he wants to control the circumstances, he loses focus on the existential matters and falls into unbalance.

This is what happens to Joseph, who tries to control the circumstances he experiences with his colleague and the students in a pseudo-omnipotent manner, believing that he can change even the

44 | THE MEANING OF THE DIVINE LAWS IN OUR LIVES

Divine Laws. When behaving this way, Joseph becomes despotic toward himself and his colleague, who he bombards energetically with his rage, but since at the same time he is restricted by the "good guy" persona he has created, he feels impotent, believing that he cannot do anything to change the situation. With these actions, Joseph immerses himself into physical and emotional imbalance, running away from existential accomplishments, in spite of the positive intention of helping.

Many people act just like Joseph, focusing on circumstantial matters, wanting to control them instead of properly guiding them, and end up distancing themselves from their own essence and losing themselves in a web of problems that take a lot of work to solve.

When Joseph nurtures the desire to change his colleague he manifests pseudo-omnipotence. Since such omnipotence is nothing more than a futile desire, he enters into sentiment of despotism. But since he is immersed in the persona of the "good guy", in the pseudo-kindness that characterizes him, he manifests this negative feeling of despotism in his body and mind, entering into a state of anxiety and developing a gastric ulcer and psoriasis, since all the aggressiveness remains in an energetic field that reaches not only his colleague's vibrational field, but also, and mainly, himself.

Despotism, therefore, is not a movement of aggression that only affects others, but is also a form of self-aggression.

As Professor Joseph keeps on feeding of all these ego-based feelings, he will progressively crystallize his persona, in a process of **pseudo-inalterability,** isolating himself from the essential matters of Life. This inner isolation produces a large void and creates, paradoxically a great evil within his own person, although his desire is to do what is good.

When Jesus says that we cannot serve two lords, God and Mammon, he is not only referring to material matters, which is how the majority of people understand it, with Mammon referring to material matters and God referring to spiritual. Any behavior in which the Spirit does not want to respect the Divine Laws is a movement toward wanting to serve two lords, even when they want to behave "well", as in the case of Professor Joseph, who, on the level of his secondary intentions creates an entirely falsified behavior, a sophism that ends up harming himself and others.

How to behave in accordance with the Divine Laws, becoming closer to the attributes of God and developing balanced virtues

Now we will analyze the actions Professor Joseph can accomplish in accordance with the Divine Laws, getting closer to the attributes of God and developing the essential virtues of Life.

For our reflections, we will use questions from *The Spirits' Book* and a message by Lazarus about Duty, studied in the previous meeting[8].

It's of utmost importance for Professor Joseph to assume an authentic posture in relation to his own life, working towards his **individualization** instead of stimulating **personalism**. By surrendering to the masquerade of his ego, he fails to fulfill the Divine Laws and distanced himself from the attributes of God.

It's only possible to fulfill the Divine Laws by developing virtues. For each Divine Law we have one or more virtues. To understand this, we can use an analogy. Let's imagine a river. So that it can exist, a series of physical laws are contemplated. There are

---

8 Author's note: We suggest that you reread the questions and message in the previous chapter.

margins, the riparian forest, and the river source that flows down due to the unlevelled terrain until it meets another river, ending up in the sea. All of these factors must work together in order for the movement of water to take place. Comparatively, the conjunction that forms the river is the Divine Law and the waters that flow into it are the virtues. For example, when we speak about the **Law of Love, Justice and Charity**, there are also the virtues of **love**, of **justice and** of **charity**; moreover, the **Law of Duty**, virtue of **duty**; **Law of Freedom**, virtue of **discernment**, etc.

The main virtue, therefore, to be developed so that Joseph can fulfill the Laws, under **The Law of Freedom**, is the virtue of **discernment**, as it allows one to *distinguish practically between good and bad*, doing everything for the benefit of everyone, as taught in question 629 of *The Spirits' Book*.

We see that the Spiritual Benefactors teach us that everything should be done for the benefit of everyone, and this includes oneself. When Joseph is concerned about changing the external circumstances, he distances himself from the idea of benefiting everyone.

Discernment is developed by asking basic questions to oneself: What should I do? What shouldn't I do? Although simple, these questions are very effective, along with these: What is in my reach and what isn't? Do I have the power the change external circumstances: people, processes, systems etc.? In all the circumstances in which we are invited to take part in an interpersonal relationship and to deal with external processes, we should use these questions as a guide to discern what we should do.

These questions are essential for Joseph, to help him to avoid wanting to control or manage the circumstances. We can turn to another Divine Law to understand how this is done: The **Law of Love Justice and Charity**. Trying to control external circumstances is neither loving, nor just or charitable toward oneself or others. This is why Joseph enters into pseudo-omnipotence/despotism and impotence.

It's imperative to develop **potency**, in other words, to work existentially on accomplishing actions in order to transform our own lives, while contributing circumstantially to the transformation of the external world. All these actions should be filtered through the virtues of **love, justice** and **charity**, virtues that are associated with discernment so that the **Law of Responsibility** can be fulfilled. We are all free to do what we want, but we are responsible for everything that we do. Therefore developing the virtue of **responsibility** is also imperative.

The conscientious commitment of all of us is to accomplish goodness to the limit of our strength. That is why we should never act with indifference, washing our hands in relation to the problems of the world in which we live. As the Spiritual Benefactors teach us in question 642 of *The Spirits' Book*, we will answer for all the evil we cause by not doing good; moreover, we should not revolt against matters that are guided by the Divine Laws.

Therefore, Joseph should not be the guardian of his colleague's inner probity, because that would be impossible, as Lazarus teaches us: *The duty of moral obligation for a human being is to itself first then towards others*, in other words, first the **existential,** second the **circumstantial.** There is no way of fulfilling the Divine Laws through others and, as obvious as this affirmation may be, there are few people who actually base their actions on it.

By trying to be guardians of other's inner probity, many people create a serious problem for themselves and create conflicts in their relationships with others, as Joseph has done, creating the types of afflictions that we studied in the previous meeting, afflictions that are totally unnecessary.

This issue is directly linked to the **Law of Progress.** Moral evolution is an individual and nontransferable process. As we evolve, we indirectly help the world to evolve, but the power of action lies only within our own Self, the immortal Spirit. Let's always remember this.

How can Professor Joseph develop the virtue of **responsibility** in synchronicity with the virtue of **conscientious duty**, acting with social responsibility, accomplishing goodness to the limit of his forces, as well as doing it without indifference as is the case with many people, or without revolting as evidenced by his previous behavior? First, Joseph should make all the necessary efforts to be an excellent teacher, presenting himself as an exemplary professional. This would be a loving, just and charitable behavior toward himself because it would make him a better person, while at the same time he could start pointing out questions for his negligent colleague to consider, such as: *Would you like it if you were treated like you're treating the students, becoming a health professional that is ill formed due to the negligence of your professors? Think about it.* After these remarks it would be necessary to let his colleague take the time to think things over.

In our professional relationships we are invited to be sowers of the seeds of love instead of taking on the role of reapers. The one who will reap the fruits from planted seeds will be the person who actually planted them, as is taught by Jesus in the Parable of the Sower[9].

This loving attitude will be just and charitable toward his colleague, who instead of receiving the destructive vibrations from Joseph, will receive positive criticism in the form of loving questioning that will encourage him to think about his attitude. Whether

9 Author's note: For greater details about the parable and its application in the human relationships, consult another one of our books titled: – Therapeutic Parables, Volume 1.

the seeds will germinate immediately or much later on, will not be any part of Joseph's responsibility but will be brought about by the Divine Laws which will bring to his colleague an awareness of the consequences of his actions so that he can reflect upon them lovingly or painfully. The choice to change will always be up to his colleague and not up to Joseph.

It's important for Joseph to always affirm to himself that he is not the guardian of the his colleague's conscience, but the **Law of Duty** and the virtue of **duty** invite him to be the guardian of his own inner probity, never of others.

In regards to the students Joseph should stop **preoccupying** himself with their bad education and their future, but should **occupy** himself in doing the best he can within his possibilities as their professor, educating them so that they may be well prepared not only technically but especially morally for the various circumstances of life.

The students are settled in waiting for Joseph to solve their problems but instead, Joseph should encourage them to avoid both their submissiveness as well as their revolt, and encourage them to question the negligent professor; to present the issue to the school board, etc. Still, it isn't Joseph who should initiate these actions but, rather, the students should do it.

By proceeding in this way, Joseph would be truly acting out of love for what is good, instead of oscillating between bad and pseudo-good, behaving according to the teachings in questions 632 of *The Spirit's Book*, doing unto others what we would like to be done unto ourselves, as is recognized in the **Law of Charity**. As the spiritual Mentors say, there is no way of having space for **sophisms of passion**, for self-deceit, when we behave in this way.

SELF-REFLECTIVE EVALUATION

• Close your eyes and connect with your inner self, in search of the content studied in this meeting.

• Analyze yourself in an authentic manner, avoiding self-deceit.

• From the content, what did you understand that applies to your life?

• Did the content studied change the way you feel about the Divine Laws in yourself? If so, what changes are these?

• What did you understand in relation to the Divine Laws, Divine Attributes and the practice of virtues to produce harmony in the interpersonal relationships at work?

• In this meeting we reflected about the existential concepts and the conscientious duty of working for our own improvement, by guiding the circumstances within the reach of our possibilities. Feel in yourself this reality. Have you been focused on the external circumstances or have you been trying to control them?

• What did you understand about the duty of guarding the inner probity of the immortal Spirit? Did you notice yourself in sync with the Law of Duty, or did you try to be the guardian of someone else's conscience, or act with indifference in relation to others?

• What is it like for you, to make efforts towards developing that conscientious duty, of emphasizing the attributes of God in your life, submitting to His Laws. Feel the possibility within yourself. How do you feel? What does it feel like to make these efforts?

- Proceeding from a deeper understanding of the meaning of the Divine Laws, in your life and developing the essential virtues as an etiquette of these Laws, has there been an amplification of the will to develop these virtues? How is this for you?

- How does it feel, by making efforts to live and practice the Divine Laws, accomplishing goodness to the limit of your forces? Do you feel that it's possible for you to make these a usual practice in your life or does some form of objection to this practice still exist?

- How do you feel about your life, in applying the content studied? Do you feel that it can improve your life in the search of self-transformation and in the acts of good deeds?

- Now, recognize yourself as the immortal Spirit you are, who brings within the divine purview the determination to evolve until reaching relative perfection, through the pure understanding of the fulfilment of the Divine Laws, through the practice of virtues and by striving to be one with God. Submerge yourself profoundly into this spiritual truth. Feel and see yourself fulfilling the Divine Laws and developing all the essential virtues of Life throughout time, feeling the loving presence of God in your life.

- Gradually, start returning to a state of alertness. Open your eyes and write down your reflections.

4th Meeting

The Divine Laws and volunteer work

part I

Objective – To reflect on the meaning of the Divine Laws in our lives in order to love, respect and integrate them into our volunteering activities.

Initial reflection – *Meditating on the meaning of the Divine Laws in our lives*

Close your eyes and connect with your inner self, in search of feeling as an immortal Spirit, a child of God, created to evolve and achieve plenitude.

• How do you feel?

• Have you surrendered yourself fully to God and His Laws?

- How have you been dealing with the Divine Laws in your volunteering activities? Have you been applying them?

- Let your thoughts and feelings flow, avoiding any masks or self-deceit. Be true to yourself, analyzing yourself with authenticity.

- Now open your eyes, returning to a state of awareness. Write down your experience: the feelings you had, the thoughts that came to mind, the sensations that you benefited from.

REFLECTIONS BASED ON SPIRITISM
QUESTIONS FOR SELF-REFLECTION

- Knowing that the Divine Laws are present in our conscience and that they exist for us to reach pure and eternal happiness, what actions can be accomplished to love and fulfill them in our volunteering activities?

- What are the practical means that we can use in order to manifest the divine attributes and the essential virtues of Life in our volunteering activities?

In this meeting, we will begin by studying the application of the Divine Laws in volunteering activities.

Volunteer work as a challenging experience to fulfill the Divine Laws

In this meeting and the ones that follow, we will study other true stories. This time around we will focus on volunteer work in a Spiritist Center. The objective is to study the case from the same perspective that was reflected upon in the second meeting, based on the proposal of question 919 of *The Spirits' Book*.

The idea is to study, in a practical manner, common occurrences that happen in many Spiritist Centers, in order to reflect on the mistakes other people have made so that we can get to know ourselves better and analyze whether we act the same way or, perhaps, engage in even worse behavior. In this manner we may improve as incarnate, immortal Spirits, invited to accomplish goodness to the limit of our strength (question 642 *The Spirits' Book*).

John is the president of a Spiritist Center that has various volunteer workers who come within his sphere of influence. He is a charismatic leader and believes that his leadership responsibility is very challenging, as there is a great need for diplomacy to fulfill this role. In John's estimation, the workers, who are all volunteers are actually doing a favor for the Spiritist Center and should be able to accomplish their tasks when and how they are able to without any demands.

For this reason, John is confronted with many difficulties in speaking to some of the directors and collaborators of the Center when he knows that they did something that diverts from the Spiritist postulates that should govern the center's activities. John believes that because they are volunteers, if something is said, they will take offence and will leave the task that they are assigned to do.

John believes that bringing errors to their attention is indicative of a lack of charity and that we should be tolerant and indulgent with regard to the deficiencies of others.

For this reason, many problems occur in the Spiritist Center, such as: mistaken explanations by during speeches and in the fraternal counseling sessions, as well as absences without prior warning, amongst other things.

When the situation becomes unsustainable, John is used to saying, in an indirect manner in the directors' meetings, that people do not collaborate in the correct manner in the activities of the Center, and says all of this with a feeling of resentment at being unjustly treated as a leader.

However, the situation remains the same, along with the worsening factor that the more dedicated workers feel unjustly treated, since John is not very clear in the board meeting. It's left up in the air as to who he is talking about, causing everyone to being led to believe that they are being judged as irresponsible, which is not true. Some of the volunteers try to tell him to take a more direct action, by speaking with those who are to blame, but everything remains the same.

Let's reflect on the case of John and the other workers of the Spiritist Center under the light of the triad[10]: Self, Immortal Spirit, and Divine Laws and God, which have already been studied in the first meeting of this module.

In relation to God, it's our duty to surrender to Him, by developing His attributes and loving, respecting and fulfilling the Divine Laws. As we have already learned, the Divine Laws are blessings of the Creator, given to us so that we can achieve ultimate happiness. Therefore, it's up to us to conquer, in relation to our true Self, which is our Immortal Spirit, the development of the essential virtues of Life.

These are the attitudes that should be carried out: **surrender** to the **blessings** of God and the **conquest** of virtues in the effective action of self-transformation, causing a virtuous cycle, where we reach for self-knowledge with a well-defined intention of existential self-improvement. By developing the essential virtues, we are able to fulfill the Divine Laws and manifest the attributes of God that reinforce the practice of virtues in a positive cycle of self- nourishment.

---

10 Authors Note: We suggest that you look at figure 3 again with its retrospective explanation in chapter one.

Now, we will try to determine if John is implementing these virtuous cycle in his current attitudes.

We can begin by reflecting on question 632 of *The Spirits' Book*: *Since we are subject to error, can't we be mistaken in our appreciation of good and bad and believe that we are doing right when, in fact, we are doing wrong?*

"Jesus has said: 'So always treat others as you would like them to treat you.' The whole of the ethical law is contained in that commandment. Make it your rule of action, and you will never go wrong."

Through his narrative, we have seen that John believes he is charitable, indulgent and tolerant with the workers of the Center. Could John at any moment have thought that he is actually acting in error towards the situation? After reflecting upon the question above, we can conclude that he probably is not. Very few people engage in the habit of reflecting upon their attitudes in a conscientious manner.

Let us analyze his case. Could it be that John is in fact, acting in accordance to the Christian precept of doing unto others that which we would like to be done unto ourselves? The Divine Law described in question 632 is the Law of Love, Justice and Charity because when we do to others that which we would like to have done unto us, we proceed with justice, love and charity toward ourselves and others.

It's essential to remember that the Divine Laws do not compete with one another. On the contrary, they support one another. If one Law is disrespected, the others are also indirectly disrespected because they function in solidarity and interdependence with one another.

In the same manner that the essential virtues of Life also support one another. Let's reflect: John says he doesn't call attention to the volunteer workers when they commit an error because he *has* to be indulgent and tolerant with them, and even more, that they are doing a favor for the Center. Is John's behavior a virtuous practice in tune with the Law of Love, Justice and Charity? Is there truly charity, indulgence and tolerance when we have an unauthentic and *passive collaborating* behavior? The virtues are interdependent and harmonious among themselves. There simply isn't a way to be charitable, and at the same time, be unauthentic and *passively supportive of wrong actions*. Therefore, what many people believe to be indulgence and tolerance is, in fact, nothing of the kind.

It is possible to develop one virtue more than others? If we consider that they are interdependent and sum up each other, then even if we have one more developed than the others, it becomes clear that it is necessary to exercise and develop the others, bringing them into balance with those that are more developed, so that we can act in a virtuous manner.

For example, in the case of John, without authenticity and frankness it's impossible to truly exercise charity, let alone indulgence and tolerance. This is why he developed pseudo-kindness, believing that he was being kind and charitable.

Analyzing the difficulties of this Spiritist Center in relation to the triad of the immortal Spirit, God and the Divine Laws, what are the main problems experienced by John and by the negligent collaborators?

Limitations of the President of the relation to divine attributes

In relation to the divine attributes John manifests the following limitations:

Attribute: Oneness
Limitation: Personalism

It's very clear to see that John cultivates the persona of a good guy, just like Professor Joseph who was studied in the previous meetings. He acts as a passive supporter of negative actions, believing that this attitude is virtuous, through a masked process of the subconscious.

When things get out of hand from the false control that he maintains, he complains at the council meeting, in an unclear manner about what is taking place. This behavior continues to make his relationship with the workers grow more superficial with each passing day.

Can Spiritist institutions function in this manner? Unfortunately, many institutions are like this, enveloped by personalism, which is cultivated to the detriment of being authentic.

Although there are some honorable exceptions, it is still a real taboo in the Spiritist movement, that important matters relating to volunteer work be discussed openly with love, charity, patience, tolerance, indulgence, affability and docility, but above all, with authenticity. The preferred method is omission because it's easier to cultivate personalism instead of developing the powers within each individual, thereby making the work in goodness a source of self-awareness and self-transformation.

In a Spiritist Organization, to accomplish works aimed at what is good and in tune with Jesus and Kardec is not a simplistic process, as many may think. It's an invitation to begin a profound process of inner transformation.

Attribute: Supreme Kindness and Justice
Limitation: Cruelty, Pseudo-Kindness and Injustice

Due to the fact that John cultivates pseudo kindness, he is more apt to make omissions and thus more apt to make mistakes in his day to day interactions. The answer to question 642 of *The Spirits' Book* says clearly that we are invited to perform good works to the limit of our strengths, and, therefore we will answer for all the wrongs that derive from all the good that was not done.

When John omits himself, individual and collective mistakes are made. This behavior creates harm to himself, to the people around him and to all the remaining workers and participants of the Spiritist Center he is a part of.

Evaluation:

Harm to himself – by not developing the essential virtues of Life, that require a continuous, patient, perseverant and disciplined effort. He chose instead to exercise pseudo-virtues that are easy to be practiced, but only cause personalism, instead of individual growth.

Harm to others (volunteer workers of the Center) – the fact that John is president of the Center gives him a great responsibility: dealing with all the volunteers with justice and kindness. As he does not open up to develop the necessary virtues, he is lacking charity, because he is not doing unto others that which he wished to be done to him, since a worker with even a minimal amount of awareness would like to be alerted when he/she is making some sort of mistake so that it can be corrected. If the workers remain unknowing, how will they change that which they do not notice to be a problem? Another harm caused by John is that of treating the problem in a generic manner in the council meetings, acting unfairly with the dedicated workers, and accusing all of them instead of being specific about the situation at hand.

Harm to the participants of the Center – as we have seen in the narrative of the case, inappropriate comments are made during the public speaking presentations and in the fraternal counseling sessions, causing harm to the participants of the Center who are seeking out more information about how Spiritism explains the existential questions of life. By receiving misguided orientations based on assumptions, they end up having an imprecise impression of Spiritism. This is the main harm produced by the dubious attitude of John. Conscientiously speaking, it's a very serious and mistaken act of leaders of Spiritist Centers who allow any anti-Spiritist information to be passed along in the name of Spiritism, the Promised Consoler.

Attribute: Immutability
Limitation: Pseudo-inalterability

The main characteristic that John derives from the practice of personalism is his pseudo-inalterability, since it concentrates on *appearing* and not on *being*. John cultivates the image of a charismatic leader, who wants to be 'okay' with everyone, and for this reason, becomes permissive, maintaining a dubious attitude, focused on the masks of the ego.

Attribute: Omnipotence
Limitation: Impotence, Pseudo-omnipotence and Despotism

Since John does not act existentially, he wishes to control the resulting circumstances[11], which is impossible to do it so. That is why John enters into a sentiment of impotence when he thinks that things are escaping his control. Because he cultivates a persona of pseudo-omnipotence and has the illusion of being in control of the circumstances, he feels unfairly treated once he realizes his impotence in controlling them, and resorts to despotism to try to assume a control which he never had.

Attribute: Omniscience
Limitation: Unconsciousness and Pseudoscience

John acts with unconsciousness because he places at risk the

---

11 Authors Note: We suggest that you record the existential and circumstantial concepts, studied in the previous chapter.

credibility of the institution that should be zealously supportive of Spiritism, by acting with omission, and causing harm, as it has already been reviewed in a previous analysis. He does not act in a malicious manner, but his omission is nevertheless, the cause of harm.

At the same time, his pseudoscientific methodology becomes clear when he undermines the precept – without charity there is no salvation -, due to the lack of a deep understanding about the real meaning of charity, as we have already explained.

Limitations of negligent employees in relation to divine attributes

In relation to the divine attributes, the negligent volunteers manifest the following limitations:

Attribute: Unicity
Limitation: Personalism

All the volunteer workers act with personalism because they believe that by simply volunteering to carry out good deeds, they are already good. They are deceiving themselves into thinking they are spiritually advanced via the masked proposal of engaging in material religious activities, since they believe that they are doing good, but in fact they are creating great harm for themselves and others.

Attribute: Supreme Attribute of Kindness and Justice
Limitation: Cruelty and Injustice

The fact that someone volunteers for a task in a Spiritist Center, makes that person as much or even more responsible for that task as they would be if they were being paid for it. Everyone assumes a conscious responsibility by accepting a task in Jesus's harvest. When they act with negligence, be it through their absence or by not qualifying themselves adequately to accomplish the volunteer activities assumed, they produce a great harm and injustice toward all those who are involved in those activities, whether they are colleagues, leaders or those who would otherwise have benefitted from the services being provided.

One of the strategies of the shadows nowadays is exactly that, to encourage people who aren't fully committed to stay in those charitable institutions. A person may remain responsible for a task but her execution of it isn't proper and ends up causing harm towards herself and towards so many others. There are many who actually think they are doing good because, after all, they are carrying out a voluntary assignment in a charitable institution. However, if those who think this way, listened to their own conscience, in Truth they would in truth, see the great harm they are committing.

Attribute: Immutability
Limitation: Volubility and Pseudo-inalterability

People who volunteer at the Spiritist Center and shirk their responsibilities without previous warning fluctuate between volubility and pseudo-inalterability, maintaining this behavior without reflecting upon the meaning of their volunteerism. They pretend to be involved in charitable work but are actually using their free will badly.

Attribute: Omnipotence
Limitation: Impotence

When someone who has voluntarily embraced a volunteer work in the name of Jesus and does not fulfill their task to the limit of their forces, they enter into their own impotence, because moral laziness is the only obstacle to the completion of any task.

Attribute: Omniscience
Limitation: Unawareness

There is an unconscious behavior in relation to life and our position as volunteers in our present reincarnation. It's the readjustment before our own consciences of the errors committed in our spiritual past. The work in Jesus' harvest on the other hand, is something that is conscientious and we ask for it before we reincarnate.

Generally speaking, those who are invited to work in the Spiritist Center have a serious commitment toward life and work as a loving manner of redemption. Not assuming this commitment in a serious manner is a very irresponsible act.

This is why Jesus teaches in the Parable of the Workers of the Last Hour[12] that many are called, but few are chosen. Our own conscience chooses us, when we act in an existential manner, accomplishing the good to the best of our abilities.

Now we will study the main Divine Laws that John and the volunteers failed to observe when they acted in a careless manner.

Law of Love, Justice and Charity: Even though they believe that they are practicing charity, John and the other volunteers are failing to exercise the Greater Law for the reasons already studied.

Law of Freedom: Instead of freedom, the Spiritist Center administrated by a permissive leader, cultivates recklessness, since freedom is intimately linked to responsibility. Recklessness, on the other hand, is the fruit of indiscipline and negligence. This is what John allows at the Center he is in charge of. Recalling the narrative, we perceive that John thinks he cannot say anything if a volunteer is absent in a task or behaves in an inappropriate manner, because in his mind that person is doing the Center a favor by working as a volunteer.

Benefiting from the Law of Freedom only truly happens when we are in tune with the greater Law and we act with love,

---

12 Author's Note: For greater details on the parable, we suggest the reading of the *Therapeutic Parables*, Volume II, published by Editora Espiritizar, of our authorship.

justice and charity. Any one of us can use our free will poorly, but we will suffer the consequences of this poor use.

Law of Duty: When someone volunteers to carry out a task, they have the conscientious duty of accomplishing it. John, as well as the negligent volunteers failed to observe this Law.

Law of Responsibility: This Law is profoundly linked to the Laws of Freedom and Duty. We are free to do what we want in our lives, including, not accomplishing tasks we accepted in the Spiritist movement, in a process of direct or indirect desertion.

In relation to the activities we accept to be involved in the Spiritist movement, there are two types of desertions linked to the Law of Responsibility.

Direct – the type of desertion in which the person leaves the task and even the Spiritist movement or Spiritism itself. This choice delays their possibilities of renewal through being involved in the work of love. They will be conscientiously responsible for all the good that was left undone, causing harm to themselves. In this case, since the deserter will be replaced by someone else, the direct desertion isn't as bad as the indirect one.

Indirect – a person neither abandons the task, nor accomplishes it in a responsible manner. The volunteer remains actively taking care of their responsibilities but in an inefficient or ineffective manner, and will of course be responsible for all the bad that derives from this attitude. It's more serious than the other, since the person remains in the task, accomplishing it in an unsatisfactory manner instead of putting all the necessary effort in to do quality work. And all of this is done in the name of Christ the Consoler.

This is the case with John and the volunteers who are acting in a negligent manner. They are responsible for all that they do, including all the harm that derives from them not doing the good to the best of their abilities.

Presently, this type of desertion has caused a lot of trouble to Spiritist Centers and the Spiritist movement as a whole, much more than the direct desertion.

Law of progress: What happens to a Spiritist Institution within the same framework implemented by John? They do not progress, remaining stagnated and delaying the advancement offered by the Promised Consoler.

There is a strategy of Organized Inferior Spirits[13] in promoting this type of institution. People who work in these organizations may think that they are doing something good but in truth are causing those places to become stagnated due to their unwillingness to do what their consciences require of them.

Nowadays there are many Spiritist Centers functioning this way. Although the Spiritism itself is indestructible, because it's directed by Superior Spirits who in their turn are directed by Jesus, the Spiritist movement itself is vulnerable, since it depends on the good will of the people who participate in it. Because many people are not alert to the need to practice the Divine Laws in their lives, we have as a result this formation of inadequate frameworks taking place in many institutions. So many activities are being implemented in a weak, inefficient and ineffective manner. Spiritism is not impeded from shining, but the Spiritist movement is seriously undermined.

Law of Labor: John and all the negligent workers disregarded the Law of Labor.

---

13 Author's Note: For more information about *this* plan, consult the book *Obsession In The Spiritist movement*, a compilation of our authorship based on the work of Manoel Philomeno de Miranda.

Let's see what is said in question 675 of *The Spirits' Book*: "*Should we understand that 'work' only applies to material occupations?* "*No; the spirit works, just as the body does. Every sort of useful occupation is work.*"

When someone accepts a volunteer task in Jesus's harvest, to be accomplished in a Spiritist institution, they are not doing a favor for the institution or for the leaders, as is commonly thought. Rather, they are doing a favor for themselves by being useful to their own inner transformation, by repaying the debts of the past and by building up credits. But they are only doing so if they are working in an efficient and effective manner, while at the same time transforming themselves into better persons, developing their virtues, fulfilling the Divine Laws and manifesting the attributes of God in their lives.

When acting in a negligent manner, serious debts are assumed by the persons own conscience because they are disregarding the invitation of the Superior Spirituality, which works in the name of Jesus, for the progress of the Promised Consoler on Earth.

As we have said previously, the Divine laws elucidate and support each other. The ones we have analyzed here are the main Laws that were disregarded in this specific case. If we search for the other laws, we will find, that in fact all of them were in fact disregarded in some way. All it takes is for the Law of Love, Justice and Charity to be disregarded and all the rest will follow.

The only Law that cannot be escaped from is the Law of Cause and Effect, because sooner or later all negligence cause painful effects for those who act in this way.

In the next meetings, we will study how John and the remaining workers can act to fulfill the Divine Laws and evolve conscientiously.

SELF–REFLECTIVE EVALUATION

- Close your eyes and connect with your inner self, reflecting on the content studied in this meeting.

- Analyze yourself in an authentic manner, avoiding self-deceit.

- From the content, what did you understand that applies in your life?

- Did the content studied change in any way how you feel about the Divine Laws? If so, what changed?

- What did you understand in relation to the Divine Laws, the Divine Attributes and the practice of virtues that occur in volunteer work that you participate in?

- What did you understand about the difference between pseudo-good and real goodness, having as a guide the precept of doing unto others that which you would like them to do to you? How does your understanding of this difference make you feel? Have your activities in the Spiritist movement been led by this guide?

- In this meeting we reflected on two types of desertions of the work of goodness: direct and indirect. Do either of these apply to you? How do you fulfill your volunteer work? Have you accomplished the good to the limit of your strength?

- In this meeting we also reflected on the importance of making efforts to reach the Essential truth and to develop the authenticity and to promote the attributes of God in our lives, while submitting to His Laws. Strive to feel this possibility within yourself. How do you feel?

- How do you feel about making efforts to live and practice all the Divine Laws in your activities as a volunteer worker? How do you accomplish this task?

- How does your life feel when applying the content studied? Do you feel that it can change your life in your search for self-transformation and in your practical activities of good deeds?

- Now, recognize yourself as the immortal Spirit you are, who brings within the divine purview the determination to evolve until reaching relative perfection, through the pure understanding of the fulfilment of the Divine Laws, through the practice of virtues and by striving to be one with God. Submerge yourself profoundly into this spiritual truth. Feel and see yourself fulfilling the Divine Laws and developing all the essential virtues of Life throughout time, feeling the loving presence of God in your life.

- Gradually, start returning to a state of alertness. Open your eyes and write down your reflections.

5th Meeting

The Divine Laws and volunteer work

part II

Objective – To reflect on the meaning of the Divine Laws in our lives, in order to love, respect and apply them in volunteer work.

Initial reflection – *Meditating on the meaning of the Divine Laws in our lives*

- Close your eyes and connect with your inner self, in search of feeling as an immortal Spirit, a child of God, created to evolve and achieve plenitude.

- How do you feel?

- Have you surrendered yourself fully to God and His Laws?

- How have you been dealing with the Divine Laws in your volunteering activities? Have you been applying them?

- Let your thoughts and feelings flow, avoiding any masks or self-deceit. Be true to yourself, analyzing yourself with authenticity.

- Now open your eyes, returning to a state of awareness.

- Write down your experience: the feelings that you had, the thoughts that came to mind, the feelings you benefited from.

REFLECTIONS BASED ON SPIRITISM
QUESTIONS FOR SELF–REFLECTION

- Knowing that the Divine Laws are present in our conscience and that they exist for us to reach pure and eternal happiness, what actions can we take in order to love and fulfill them in our volunteering activities?

- What are the practical means that can be used to develop virtues, fulfilling the divine attributes in our volunteering activities?

In this meeting we will continue to study the application of the Divine Laws in volunteer work activities.

How to accomplish a volunteering activity in a spiritist institution, within a christian proposal
part I

In the last meeting we studied the case of the president of the Spiritist Center, John, who has to deal with many challenging experiences in his role as director of the Center, especially in his leadership activities. John acts as a typical passive leader, failing to initiate corrective leadership measures at the right time while hoping that the ongoing activities will develop "peacefully" by themselves.

Before we initiate further analysis, we suggest that you re-read the narrated case in the previous chapter.

Initially, we will study what Jesus says about the experience lived by John and the other collaborators of the Spiritist Center.

We start with a Christian precept that is often cited: John, 8:32 – *Know the truth and the truth will set you free.*

Every time we do not reach for the Truth, we disregard the Divine Laws, especially the Law of Freedom because according to Jesus's teachings, there will only be real freedom once we embrace our responsibility to know, feel and live the Truth, which encompasses the Laws established by God to organize the Universe.

By using the Law of Freedom incorrectly, the immortal Spirit is not truly free because it becomes responsible for the mistaken acts that it has practiced and enslaves itself to the pain and the suffering until it learns to use the Law of Freedom with discernment and in harmony with the Laws of Love, Justice and Charity.

Both John and the other volunteer workers, who act with negligence, are distancing themselves from the Truth, although John keeps on deceiving himself into thinking he is being charitable, indulgent and tolerant.

It's easier to live the *lie of personalism*. Why does this happen? The answer becomes clear once we realize that evolution is only possible if we are willing to embrace the Law of Labor. Fueling personalism in a psychological game of make believe is much easier, pretending that charity, indulgence, tolerance etc. are being practiced. To be *seemingly* virtuous is infinitely easier than to actually be virtuous. There is plenty of moral laziness to go around. When behaving like this, one puts aside the Truth while living a lie.

Thus, without attuning, identifying with, and above all loving the Law of Labor we cannot free ourselves from past negative traits. For that, one must make continuous efforts, exercising patience, perseverance and discipline in order to move ahead towards the Truth, bringing it to our hearts through the fulfillment of the Divine Laws and through the practice of virtues. One must understand that freedom is not an easy process and that there are many things needed in order for it to be achieved.

We are invited to carry out plenty of work in our inner world so that we may self-transform. This is the Truth that many still run away from in our Spiritist movement.

In continuing to study the Gospel of Jesus, we see in Matthew, 12: 34-37, what the master says about interpersonal communication:

"You brood of vipers, how can you who are evil say anything good? For the mouth speaks what the heart is full of. A good man brings good things out of the good stored up in him, and an evil man brings evil things out of the evil stored up in him. But I tell you that everyone will have to give account on the Day of Judgment for every empty word they have spoken. For by your words you will be acquitted, and by your words you will be condemned."

Jesus frequently communicates through symbols and images. Heart is used here as a symbol for feelings. We will place in our spoken words the feelings that we have in abundance in our hearts. If our hearts are full of love, we will speak with love, if full of hate, we will express this hate, if full of false concepts, based on pseudo-love, we will express it in an unauthentic manner, as did John.

In the verses that follow, the Master Jesus makes clear the meaning of the previous verse, by referring to the *good and the evil treasure in the heart*. So, if our hearts are filled with good treasure, we will take from it good things when we communicate with people; however, if our hearts are full of *bad treasure*, we will communicate the bad treasure that we are nurturing.

What is the meaning of the *Day of Judgment?* It's the day of our disincarnation, in which our conscience goes under review, in an automatic manner, measuring all that we accomplished, which is all of that which we spoke of and felt, all of what we did with our treasure during our whole life, tallying up in split seconds through our mind, so that we can assess the values of what we have contributed in our lives.

If we find in this balance many useless words, words that come out of a bad treasure, those which were less dignified, that were used to cause harm, or simply were not used to accomplish good deeds within the limits of our capabilities as per question 642 of *The Spirits' Book*, already analyzed in this book, our conscience will condemn us. On the other hand, we may find good words to justify ourselves: *Because by your words you will be justified, and by your words you will be condemned.*

Who will absolve or condemn us? We, ourselves, because we carry the Divine Laws in our own conscience, which recommends the practice of good, love, justice and of charity.

If we have acted in accordance with our conscience, reaching for the *good words in the treasure of our hearts*, we will be at ease, living in the spiritual dimension with the moral integrity we already possess in the physical dimension. Nevertheless, if we are not attentive to make sure our hearts produce *good treasure*, we will condemn ourselves to atone for our debts in subsequent incarnations.

The communication centered in the good treasure is centered on the human being who is in harmony with others, since it's based on the Greater Law of the Universe, the Law of Love, Justice and Charity, that drives the being into producing goodness through acts and words.

A balanced interpersonal communication goes through a process of directly addressing conflicts, rather than the disguising them, as John did when he chose not to individually address the problems created by the volunteer workers who acted with negligence. John tried through omission to avoid conflicts, and instead, ended up creating a cycle of conflicts, turning an environment that should have been peaceful into one where offence overthrew the prospect of peace, and intensified the discord that was already there, through the use of generalizations in his criticisms that placed all the workers on the same level.

We fall back again on the teachings of Jesus to analyze how the Master used to recommend the resolution of conflicts.

In Matthew, 10:34, Jesus said: *"Do not suppose that I have come to bring peace to the earth. I did not come to bring peace to the earth. I did not come to bring peace, but a sword."* In Luke, 12:51- *"Do you think I came to bring peace on earth? No, I tell you, but division."* In john, 14:27, Jesus says: *"Peace I leave with you; my peace I give you. I do not give to you as the world gives. Do not let your hearts be troubled and do not be afraid."*

In these verses Jesus elaborates upon the question of conflicts and how to truly resolve them. Jesus is considered the Prince of Peace. It seems, then, incoherent that He says that He did not come to bring the peace, but the *sword and division*. This inconsistency only exists when we analyze the verse literally without noting the profound meaning behind the symbols.

By saying that He came to bring the *sword or division*, what does Jesus want to teach? The key to understanding the apparently combative content is in the verses written by John the apostle, in which the Master says that he left us His *peace*. What is the peace of Jesus? His peace is totally centered in love and compassion. Is this the peace of the world? No. Why? Because the values that are still fostered in the world are egocentric false. It's a make-believe peace, marked by deception, made in the armistices of governmental chambers, without there really being any friendship between the involved nations. This is what happens, for example, in Europe today. United though economic matters, the populations of different countries only tolerate one another, living within a framework of mental warfare. The physical sword no longer exists, but the mental-emotional one surely does.

Why does this happen? Because all this peace did not pass through the division, or through the *sword* referred to by Jesus. Within a divine perspective, what is signified by division or the sword? The symbols have the same meaning: the resolution of conflicts. If the conflict does not go through the sword, it's only being concealed and the ill within the relationship remains hidden, without being resolved.

It's only possible to solve conflicts by opting for conscious choices instead of an easy way out, in which personalism predominates instead of individualization, which we should reach for to the limit of our strengths.

How can we do this in the Spiritist Center? We will focus on the communication in the Spiritist Center, the object of our study in this case. The reflections that we have made here can be extended to the family and other social relationships.

As we have seen, by saying that He *came to bring division or the sword and not peace,* Jesus is referring to the construction of inner peace and especially to the peace that can be fostered in our interpersonal relationships, which requires a lot of work from us.

In other passages of the Gospel, Jesus teaches us a method for this. He tells us in Matthew, 18:15 to 17:

> If your brother or sister sins, go and point out their fault, just between the two of you. If they listen to you, you have won them

over. But if they will not listen, take one or two others along, so that 'every matter may be established by the testimony of two or three witnesses. If they still refuse to listen, tell it to the church; and if they refuse to listen even to the church, treat them as you would a pagan or a tax collector.

The text is clear and has some very significant nuances for us to reflect upon. Jesus offers an authentic method of personal inter-relationship in institutions. We will apply the teachings proposed by Jesus to the environment of the Spiritist Center administered by John, and, by extension, to all Spiritist institutions.

In the first stage the person who did something wrong is called in private and spoken with. If she listens, then the problem is resolved. There isn't anyone who is exempted from making mistakes. But if the person does not notice the mistakes committed, someone should call their attention to that fact. This is what John should have done. Instead, he never pretended that nothing was happening, allowing the problems to accumulate until he was forced to take action. Then, when action was finally taken, John did not clarify the reason as to why those measures were taking place. Another mistake was to tell people who were not directly related to the matter about the intricacies of it.

If the person in need of correction continues with the same mistaken posture, Jesus tells us to call upon *witnesses* to participate in the conversation. Why *witnesses?* Witnesses are needed so the person does not allege, later on, that they were treated in an unfair manner and also so that the fair and loving words can be confirmed by the witnesses. This avoids the playing out of so-called he said she said scenarios that are so common in such organizations, because the matters at hand will be resolved in a collective manner. The objective is to create a truly harmonious work environment for all instead of one that just looks to be harmonious, as is commonly done.

Within an organization's environment for example, the vice-president and the area director can be asked to speak with the person in question. If the person listens, the situation is resolved. On the other hand, it may become necessary for the organization to present a united front; the *unite the church* comes into play. In this case, the person is asked to be present before a session of the board of directors, where the case will be analyzed and clearly explained to the person, who will then be asked to seriously reflect on and consider changing their behavior. If the person listens, the question is resolved, but if this person remains stubbornly resistant, then Jesus recommends considering the person as a Gentile or publican. These are very important symbols. Let's reflect upon them.

The Gentiles in those days were the None-Jews who did not understand the essential meaning behind the belief in only one God. Publicans were the tax collectors for the Roman Empire. When Jesus said to consider the person in question as equivalent to the *Gentile and the publican*, he means that this person is still not unable to recognize the Truths of Life, no matter what their nationality may be. The majority of Jews behaved as if they were Gentiles, not understanding Jesus's proposal.

The meaning of this passage as it applies to today's Spiritist movement is that people who aren't ready for such responsibilities should not be kept as workers in Spiritist organizations. What we need are volunteer workers who are focused on, and contributing towards the establishment of the Kingdom of God on Earth.

Obviously, this does not mean that perfect workers are required, but rather, that workers are needed who truly want to perfect themselves and to contribute, transforming themselves into better people, and helping others to do the same.

Many who are used to personalism may say that such views represent a lack of charity. Let's reflect: truly, Jesus taught us that those who are well aren't the ones who need doctors, but patients need to desire to get healthy, otherwise, how can they look after other patients? The Spiritist worker should be one who wants to be healthy, and when they are a little better, they are able to start helping other people who are even more ill. Therefore, when Jesus says to consider them as Gentiles and publicans, it's because those individuals still aren't whiling to become healthy and although we are to respect their free will we cannot allow their bad use of it to cause harm to others. There is no way to force anyone to truly serve.

At this present moment these individuals can only be mere participants in the ORGANIZATION, which is the only way for them to avoid causing harm to the group. That status can change once they show an interest in their personal growth within the spectrum of love.

This approach is still a major taboo in the Spiritist movement, because we continue undermining, in the name of charity, falsifying the message of Christ, thus causing harm to the Spiritist Cause. It's exactly what John does with his group of workers. By causing harm to Spiritism we distance ourselves from the proposal of Jesus and Kardec, and this is seen in many Spiritist Centers where people conduct themselves inappropriately during public speeches, speak absurdities while performing fraternal counselling services, and absent themselves without warning nor without asking for someone to cover for them. They also tend to impose their ways of thinking onto others, and their views are usually distanced from Spiritist teachings.

If we were more authentic, more Christian, the Spiritist movement would in far better shape by now. For this reason we have so many individuals taking advantage of the Spiritist movement, occupying many positions, while only a few are actually serving Jesus and working to the best of their abilities in the movement formed by Spiritist institutions.

To live the teachings of Jesus, our relationships must be authentic. Very few people are truly authentic. The majority prefer to pretend that everything is okay, creating the make-believe peace, as we presently see amongst nations around the world. We tend to act as John: We cannot *speak openly* because it might *cause offence to others*. By doing this, however, we create false relationships, and also undermine the work done in the Spiritist movement, a work that should be done with the greatest possible care in order to create the greatest possible quality, because it re-lives the Gospel of Jesus, in Spirit and Truth. But what is even more serious is that many unauthentic individuals mistakenly think they are behaving with charity, indulgence and tolerance, to their own detriment, as we have already examined.

What is the problem in reaching out to someone who we have a difficult relationship with or who is causing a problem for a group we participate in, and saying the truth in a loving way, centered in love, compassion and in Christian authenticity?

Jesus recommends that we should not feel disquieted in our hearts, nor should we torment ourselves. If we are reaching for his peace, should there be any fear of saying the Truth? No! Therefore, why is this frankness and authenticity so uncommon? The problem is that since personalism is our most common trait, we confuse authenticity and frankness with the rudeness of the evident ego, or simply assume the posture of the masked ego and pretend that nothing is happening. Behaving this way, we become passive accomplices with the wrongdoers so that we do not have to make a decision that asks for courage and determination.

Rudeness is a part of an egocentric and individualistic persona, practiced by people who will say anything they think to someone else's face, even if they know it's going to hurt them, whereas authenticity and frankness shine like a diamond. Let's imagine an

enormous and beautiful diamond being offered to someone. It represents the virtue of authenticity and frankness, the truth that we
offer others. Now, imagine that diamond being thrown in someone's face. That is rudeness, an egocentric behavior of someone
that throws the truth in someone else's face, with the intention of
hurting them and without offering them the opportunity to reflect
upon the real values of life.

In many Spiritist Centers, it happens as in the case studied.
A person causes intrigue, behaves inappropriately as a Spiritist public speaker or counselor, does not carry out the duties that they
have committed to etc., and no one makes an effort to alert them.
It seems as if approaching a volunteer to discuss their shortcomings
is completely off-limits, as we are afraid they might take offense
and quit being a volunteer. Instead of having a dialogue about what
is taking place, many undermine the work of Christ, without having the courage to be authentic, and without passing the conflicts
through *the sword*, in order to create the true peace.

As we said many times, this permissive practice is allowed in
the name of sublime virtues. It's a very common habit in the Spiritist
movement, although Jesus has taught in Matthew, 5:37; *All you need
to say is simply 'Yes' or 'No'; anything beyond this comes from the evil one.*

What is the virtue explained by Jesus in this verse? Authenticity. When we say yes needing to say no, and vice versa, we create
evil. This is what Jesus teaches us. It's important to remember that
He is the Model and Guide of Humanity and whom we should
truly follow.

If to be charitable, indulgent and tolerant, we give up frankness, and act with inauthenticity, hiding the truth, our actions will
create evil, as the Master vehemently taught us. We are saying yes to the
others, but by omission we'll become accomplices with their wrong-
doing and refrain from exercising charity, indulgence or tolerance.

In this respect, it's essential to remember another lesson about truth that should not be hidden. Let's look at Luke, 8:16: *"No one lights a lamp and hides it in a jar or puts it under a bed. Instead, he puts it on a stand, so that those who come in can see the light."*

In the same way that virtues support one another, never competing amongst themselves, egocentric sentiments also come together. The practice of inauthenticity connects with passive complicity and, with time, it creates great ills due to omission, such as when we refuse to say phrases like: "No, this should not be done this way. As per Christian teachings the right way of doing it's so and so, *and when you accepted to accomplish this task, you made a commitment with your own conscience; you are not doing any favors to the board of the Spiritist* Center *when you commit to a task in the Spiritist movement, but, instead, you are receiving an invitation to rehabilitate yourself before Life. When you don't honor your commitments, you deny accepting an invitation Life is making for you to take part in the works of Goodness. This behavior causes harm to yourself and to the dissemination of the Spiritism.*

How many Spiritist leaders act in this manner? Sadly, there are still very few. The majority of them still complain about the people who do not cooperate, as John did, but remain passive, causing great harm to the Spiritist movement.

When we get involved in *passive collaborating* behaviors in the Spiritist Center, we cause damage to the group as a whole, because we distance the Spiritist Center from the Cause, which encompasses the Gospel of Jesus and the Spiritism.

The ethical principle of every Christian who offers good things from the good treasure of their heart, constitutes itself in the practice and application of the Law of Love, Justice and Charity extracted from the following two precepts: in Matthew, 22:37 and 39 – Jesus replied: *"Love the Lord your God with all your heart and with*

all your soul and with all your mind. This is the first and greatest commandment. And the second is like it: *'Love your neighbor as yourself.'*
And in Matthew, 7:12 – *"So in everything, do to others what you would have them do to you, for this sums up the Law and the Prophets."*

These verses reflect the essence of the Law of Love, Justice and Charity. The practice of this Law allows us to develop loving and authentic interpersonal communications in Spiritist Centers.

We return to the question of passive complicity, previously mentioned. If we reflect, based on the Greater Law, we will notice how much this practice is harmful. Is passive collaborating and obscuring the truth, by any stretch of the imagination, a loving motion towards ourselves and others? No! Is it fair? Also no! Is it Charitable? No! If we were unknowingly making mistakes while performing a serious task, wouldn't we want someone to alert us, even if, at first, we became resentful towards that person? Knowing the profound lesson of the "lamp" placed under the bushel, we would obviously wish to be alerted to the error, as it's established in the Greater Law.

So that a communication that is centered in Christian authenticity takes place, it's essential that we practice to enter into contact with energies of love that are present in the Essential Being that we are, so that when dealing with others, we know how to detect the potential of love that is also present in them.

SELF-REFLECTIVE EVALUATION

- Close your eyes and enter into contact with yourself in essence, exploring the content studied.

- Analyze yourself with authenticity, avoiding self-deceit

- From the content, what did you understand that applies to your life?

- Has the content studied changed the way that you feel about the Divine Laws in yourself? If so, what changed?

- What did you understand in relation to the Divine Laws, the divine attributes and the practice of virtues that apply to the volunteer work in which you participate?

- In this meeting we reflected upon the concept of authenticity and frankness. Connect with your inner self, making an effort to feel these virtues? Starting from a more profound understanding of the Divine Laws in the volunteer work place and the development of the essential virtues as a principle of these Laws, has there been an amplification of the will to develop these virtues? What does this mean for you?

- In this meeting we reflected on the importance of making efforts to reach for the Essential Truth so that we can manifest the attributes of God in our lives, by submitting to His Laws. Reach within to feel this possibility in yourself. How do you feel? What is it like for you to make these efforts?

- In this meeting, we have also reflected on how we should behave in interpersonal relationships in Spiritist institutions. How do you evaluate your relationships? Are they in tune with the Christian proposal or not?

• What is it like for you to make efforts to satisfy all the Divine Laws in the activities that constitute your volunteer work? What is it like, for you to make these efforts?

• How do you feel about your life after applying the content studied? Do you feel that it can change your life for the better, in the search for self-transformation and in your efforts to carry out good deeds?

• Now, recognize yourself as the immortal Spirit you are, who brings within the divine purview the determination to evolve until reaching relative perfection, through the pure understanding of the fulfilment of the Divine Laws, through the practice of virtues and by striving to be one with God. Submerge yourself profoundly into this spiritual truth. Feel and see yourself fulfilling the Divine Laws and developing all the essential virtues of Life throughout time, feeling the loving presence of God in your life.

• Gradually, start returning to a state of alertness. Open your eyes and write down your reflections.

6th Meeting

The Divine Laws and volunteer work

part III

Objective – To reflect on the meaning of the Divine Laws in our lives, in order to love, respect and apply them in volunteer work.

Initial reflection – *Meditating on the meaning of the Divine Laws in our lives*

- Close your eyes and connect with your inner self, in search of feeling as an immortal Spirit, a child of God, created to evolve and achieve plenitude.

- How do you feel?

- Have you surrendered yourself fully to God and His Laws?

- How have you been dealing with the Divine Laws in your volunteering activities? Have you been applying them?

- Let your thoughts and feelings flow, avoiding any masks or self-deceit. Be true to yourself, analyzing yourself with authenticity.

- Now open your eyes, returning to a state of awareness.

- Write down your experience: the feelings that you had, the thoughts that came to mind, the feelings from which you benefited.

REFLECTIONS BASED ON SPIRITISM
QUESTIONS FOR SELF-REFLECTION

- Knowing that the Divine Laws are present in our conscience and that they exist for us to reach pure and eternal happiness, what actions can we take to love and fulfill them in our volunteering activities?

- What are the practical means that can be used to manifest the divine attributes and the essential virtues of Life in our volunteer work?

In this meeting we will continue to study the application of the Divine Laws in volunteer work activities.

How to accomplish a volunteering activity in a spiritist institution, within a christian proposal
part II

In the past meetings we studied the case of the president of the Spiritist Center and his volunteer workers. In this chapter we will continue to study the same case.

Before we begin, we suggest that you re-read the case, which is narrated in chapter 4.

We will start our reflections with the text of *The Gospel according to Spiritism*, chapter X, items 19 to 21:

Since no one is perfect, should we conclude that nobody has the right to be critical of other people?

Certainly not, since each of you should be working for the progress of everyone else, and especially of those who've been placed in your care. But when you do criticize, do it in moderation, trying your best to be helpful. Don't do it, as frequently happens, because you take a secret pleasure in berating someone. If this is your motive, your criticism will simply be an instance of malice. When you have to make a critical observation, do so in a way consistent with the law of love, being as considerate as possible. Be careful, too, that the criticism you levy at someone else can't also be directed at you. You should determine first whether or not you deserve the very censure you plan to give. – Saint Louis (Paris, 1860).

St. Louis is very clear by affirming that our conscientious duty is to work *for the progress of everyone else, and especially of those who've been placed in your care.* This is an alert to leaders in whatever positions they occupy, fathers and mothers in families, presidents of Spiritist Centers, directors of Companies etc.

As the spiritual Mentor teaches, when bringing something to someone's attention has a *useful purpose*, it's a duty to be undertaken in a charitable manner, with all possible care. Therefore, everything we've reflected upon in the previous meetings with regards to John's actions is within this useful objective. Working for the good of all, including those who are making mistakes, creates the opportunity for adjusting their behavior, because they may be acting mistakenly due to their ignorance of the Truth.

To maintain a person in ignorance is neither loving, nor just, nor charitable. And if the person does not act through ignorance, after exhausting all the resources, as the Master himself guides us to do and as studied in the previous meeting, we should *treat them as Gentiles*, in other words, distance them from the task because they are still not ready to truly serve in Jesus's Field. They may be allowed to help once again once, after having matured enough to desire to humble their pride and tame their rebelliousness.

Another important question that Saint Louis points out is in regard to self-evaluation. Before calling anyone's attention to a perceived error, the leaders should self-analyze to see if they are not also acting in a censurable manner, like John, who, while acting irresponsibly himself, calls the workers irresponsible.

Is it wrong to notice others' imperfections when this doesn't benefit them, even though you don't disclose anything about them?

Everything depends on your intention. Certainly you aren't prohibited from seeing wrong where it exists. It would be very inopportune to see only good everywhere, as such as illusion would hinder your progress. The mistake occurs when you use your observation in such a way that harms your neighbor and needlessly discredits him or her in the eyes of others. This is even more objectionable when you do it simply to give vent to your spite or to get satisfaction from finding fault with others. It is not inappropriate, however, to analyze someone else's imperfections as a means of furthering your own improvement, that is, to study their failings as long as nothing about the person is disclosed. This is the method of a thoughtful person, who, by observing individual cases, is able to better understand human behavior. – Saint Louis (Paris, 1860).

When we observe someone making a mistake, and that mistake is only affecting the person itself, causing no harm to others, should we do something about it? No, in this case we should only observe to learn from the mistakes of others.

If intervention is within our reach, due to a certain close-ness we may have with the person, suggestions could be made to alert them, and this would be charity at work. Furthermore, that is exactly what we would want others to do for us if we were are in a state of consciousness elevated enough to be open to suggestions from others.

> *21. Are there times when it's right to disclose the wrongdoing of others?* This is a very delicate question. Answering it requires that we reason from a space of genuine love. If a person's faults only harm him- or herself, there's no use in spreading word of them. If, however, these shortcomings might harm others, the interests of the majority outweigh those of a single person. According to circumstances, it may even become a duty to expose hypocrisy and lies, just as it is preferable that one person fall than for many to become his or her victims. In such cases, you have to weigh the total sum of the advantages and disadvantages. In such a case, one must weigh the sum of the advantages and disadvantages. – Saint Louis (Paris, 1860).

In this passage Saint Luis talks about a matter related to the group as a whole, as in the case of a Spiritist Center, where it is inadmissible for a person to be absent from a commitment with-out informing anyone so that they may be substituted, or doing speeches based on their own opinions instead of Spiritist teachings, as it happened to the Center administered by John. In this case the majority remains negatively affected because of the minority.

We studied in the previous meeting a method offered by Jesus Himself, which gives guidance for the criteria a leader should use when needing to alert someone about their wrongful actions.

Now let's study a method to be used to alert a person when they are causing harm to a whole group as in a Spiritist Center for example.

We will use the reflections of a text of *The Gospel According to*

Spiritism, chapter IX, item 6, Message *affability and kindness*, of the Spirit Lazarus:

> Good will toward your fellow human beings, the result of loving your neighbor, reveals itself in the form of warmth and kindness. Don't imagine, however, that you can always trust appearances. Education and worldly experience can give someone a thin veneer of courteousness that very much looks like these qualities. In fact, many people who seem to be good-natured are only wearing masks, as some people wear expensive clothes, to cover up moral shortcomings. The world is full of these people. They have a smile on their lips but poison in their hearts. They appear mild as long as nothing upsets them; but provoke them a little and they bite. They are eloquent and golden-tongued when they speak with you face to face; behind your back, the same tongues turn into poison darts.
>
> [...]
>
> To have milk and honey flowing from your lips isn't enough. Your heart has to correspond with the feelings you express or you're simply being a hypocrite. On the other hand, people whose friendliness and mildness are not a mere pretense never find themselves leading contradictory lives because they're the same both in society and in private. They know that, even though it might be possible to deceive people, no one can deceive God. – Lazarus (Paris, 1861).

Often times, authenticity and frankness are confused with rudeness. As we have studied, virtues complement one another, never competing amongst each other. As we have seen, authenticity is to say *yes* in the time that *yes* is meant to be said and *no* when it's time to say *no*, remembering that *whatever passes this becomes evil*, as Jesus teaches.

However, the Master did not teach us to say a rude *no* or a sugar-coated *yes*, because then there would be hypocrisy, as Lazarus teaches. Authenticity should be benevolent and delivered with affability and kindness; otherwise, it's no longer a Christian virtue. As we have seen in the previous chapter, authenticity is like a diamond and should be presented with gentleness, not thrown in a person's face.

Affability and docility are the guides of authenticity and of frankness, so that we do not do wrong while thinking we are doing good, by becoming acceptant of errors, believing that we are being charitable and indulgent as did John. In this case the virtue is inauthentic and, as Lazarus states, although *seemed to be good-natured is only wearing masks.*

Now we will study what charity and indulgence are, and how John used them as justification for his behavior. In doing that he was actually only disguising his passively collaborative behavior.

Let's examine the meaning of this ego-based vice. Inaction in the face of wrong behavior is *an act of passive collaboration, which transforms the one who fails to act into an accomplice. It can take the form of noticing some wrongdoing is being done by others, and doing nothing to block it, even though one has the power to do so.*

John's inaction fits perfectly into this concept, since he is the person who has the greatest power in the Spiritist Center, a power given to him by an election, a power to put an end to the problem presented in this case.

John, therefore, has a dual commitment, first towards those whom elected him trusting that he would administrate with his conscience as it should be done in any Spiritist organization, and second toward all those who use the services offered by the Spiritist Center he coordinates.

What did Jesus really mean when he used the words "love" and "charity"?

"Compassion for everyone, tolerance for the imperfections of others, and forgiveness of all offenses."

Love and compassion are complements of the law of justice. To love our neighbor is to do him or her all the good in our power, all that we wish might be done for ourselves.

According to Jesus, compassion is not restricted to giving money to the needy. It relates to all our relationships, regardless of rank and social position.

Charity is the result of our acting with benevolence in all our endeavors. Benevolence is the act of practicing good deeds. When the spiritual Mentors cite benevolence with all, what are they clarifying? They are saying that benevolence should encompass the totality, starting with the person who is being benevolent, who should act with love, justice and charity towards themselves and towards all those involved in their lives.

In the case of the Spiritist Center led by John, it involves himself, the careless workers, the dedicated ones that are disgruntled, and those who visit the Center, who are also harmed as they are exposed to distortions of Spiritist teachings without having the tools to discern about the truthfulness of what is being taught. In order for it to be considered charity, benevolence should be practiced towards everyone without distinction.

We notice that John is very distant from this practice, as it should never be established by choosing to ignore the imperfections of others when they affect the whole group, and that is exactly what is taking place in in John's case.

Due to the common practice of using psychological masks in society, the failure to address a problem is confused with indulgence. Understandably, it's not possible to demand perfection from others in the work they do. None of us are perfect. However, the posture of perfecting should be stimulated in all of us, and that includes learning from our mistakes and continuing to work, accomplishing benevolence to the limit of our capabilities. Acting in a any other way than that is to aid and abet that which is wrong, and should not be mistaken for the practice of indulgence.

In the case studied, John claims he did not say anything to the negligent volunteers so that they would not become offended, What is this notion of feeling offended really about? It's pride hiding behind a mask. A person who nourishes rebelliousness and pride becomes easily offended, feels resentment for anything that contradicts their self-love, and will not admit that they bring imperfections to be worked on. The decisions to avoid discussion of important issues does not in truth, have anything to do with charity.

This type of behavior is self-deceitful and should be given new meaning so that it does not happen more often in our Spiritist Centers, which should be truly Christian. All of us are being invited to act in accordance with the way that Jesus, the Model and Guide of Humanity, would act.

Let's see the true meaning of indulgence towards others imperfections. We will study *The Gospel According to Spiritism*, Chapter X Items 16, 17 and 18, a summary of the messages of *Joseph, A protector Spirit; John, Bishop of Bordéus and Dufêtre, Bishop of Nevers*, which are all about indulgence.

> Spiritists, today we would like to talk about tolerance, that pleasant brotherly feeling that each of you should hold toward other people, but which all too often is little in evidence.
> Tolerance takes no notice of the defects of others; or if it does, it refrains from talking about or disclosing them. To the contrary, tolerance tries to keep those defects that it alone knows about out of the sight of others. Moreover, if ill-disposed people do discover someone else's defects, tolerance always has a ready and plausible explanation for mitigating these defects. We don't mean here the kind of excuse that only seems to gloss over the fault while in fact making it more obvious.
> Tolerance never dwells on the defects of others unless it's to offer

help, and even then will try to do it in the most gentle manner. Tolerance never makes shocking statements or reproaches anyone; instead, it offers advice, usually in a tactful way.

Support the strong of character and encourage them to keep going. Strengthen the frail and show them the love of God, Who takes into account even the smallest degree of regret for a misguided act. Help everyone see the Angel of Repentance, who stretches out her white wings over humanity's shortcomings, as if she wanted God not to see them. Acknowledge Infinite Mercy, and never fail to say to God through thought and, above all, through actions, "Forgive us our debts, as we also have forgiven our debtors." Understand the meaning of these sublime words fully. Not only is their literal sense admirable, so is the guidance they contain.

Dear friends, be critical of yourselves, but always tolerant of others' weaknesses. This is the practice of a saintly compassion, a way of life which, unfortunately, not enough people embrace. Everyone has negative tendencies to overcome, faults to correct, and bad habits to change. Everyone has a burden to get rid of before climbing the mountain called Progress. Why, then, do you seem to have an extra sense that lets you spot your neighbor's faults but blinds you when it comes to your own? When will you stop taking notice of the small speck in your brother's or sister's eye, and instead, pay attention to the plank in your own? This plank is what blinds you and causes you to move from one failure to another. Believe what we, your spiritual kindred, are telling you. Every man and woman, proud enough to think of him- or herself as superior in virtue and merit to their brothers and sisters, is foolish and will be held accountable by Divine Justice. In its true character, compassion is always modest and mild. It doesn't dwell on a person's defects but strives to rouse better qualities. The human heart may still be a pit of passions, but hidden in its innermost recesses are the seeds of good, the life force of the spirit.

The Spiritist Doctrine is a source of blessings and comfort. Those who know it and who benefit from the uplifting teachings that are delivered from God's messengers, are indeed happy. For them, the pathway is illuminated. Along it, they can read the signposts that point them to the final goal of the journey. The signs call for putting love into action, for loving with all one's heart, for loving others like self. In short, we should extend unconditional love to everyone, and to God above all, for in our love for God we find a synthesis of all our responsibilities as human beings. For this reason, the practice of love is God's supreme Law.

Let's reflect on this synthesis of messages Allan Kardec compiled in the same chapter in which St Louis answers the three questions about others mishaps, as studied previously

Indulgence is a virtue intimately linked to the respect one has for free will, but a respect that does not collaborate with the wrongdoing of others, especially when it affects many others.

When Jesus instruct us, in the passage studied in the previous meeting, to treat those who do not want to recognize their faults as a publicans and Gentiles, what is He suggesting? Respect for the free will of others, since there is no way of forcing others to evolve. We are invited to respect someone else's right not to evolve. However, if the faults of others harm a group, we should take action to stop their actions, since the use of a Law such as of the Law of Freedom should not overshadow the other Laws, such as the Law of Responsibility and above all the Laws of Love, Justice and Charity. If the downfall of the whole is permitted, instead of indulgence we will be exercising negligence and passive collaboration.

Tolerance takes no notice of the defects of others; or if it does, it refrains from talking about or disclosing them. In the text studied, indulgence is a virtue that invites us to refrain from announcing the wrong in others, and to refrain from acting malevolently by speaking about them behind their backs.

In the Spiritist Center administered by John, there was a lot of gossip around the volunteers who were neglecting their obligations, and even John himself, as president, would also gossip about it. Without saying anything directly to the negligent volunteers, John would only make generic accusations during the board of director meetings. Nevertheless, John said that the reason he would not approach those volunteers directly is that he wanted to be indulgent and charitable towards them.

Tries to keep those defects that it alone knows about out of the sight of others. What is the spiritual Mentor referring to? Is it fault that harms the whole or one that only harms the person himself? It cannot be a fault that can only be known and harms the person himself if it involves a worker who is absent without notice from an activity at a Spiritist Center, because everyone becomes aware of their negligence.

Tolerance never dwells on the defects of others unless it's to offer help, and even then, will try to do it in the gentlest manner. Tolerance never makes shocking statements or reproaches anyone; instead, it offers advice, usually in a tactful way.

This paragraph is directly related to what we are working on. Let's reflect: Does the board of the Spiritist Center, along with its framework of volunteers, offer a service? Yes, it's a service of great value in Jesus's field.

It's essential that all of those involved exercise great zeal in the performance of this service, but that does not involve only those who are just regular attendees at the Center, mainly, it has to do with the inner transformation of the workers themselves, who can accomplish this by doing great work in Jesus' field. Thus, alerting the blameworthy workers with affability and kindness, as we have studied, without censuring them, but instead giving them specific suggestions as to what they can make better, is the duty of charity and indulgence.

Support the strong of character and encourage them to keep going. Strengthen the frail and show them the love of God, Who takes into account even the smallest degree of regret for a misguided act; show to all that the angel of penitence, extending its white wings over human faults, hides them from the look of those who cannot tolerate what is impure.

In a Spiritist Center, we are all Jesus' guests, but mainly to what end? What is the main objective of being in the Spiritist movement? Could it be to help others? No, the main invitation we receive is the opportunity to transform ourselves as people who work directly in the Spiritist Center.

So, generally speaking, what should be the greatest focus of attention in Spiritist institutions? Should it be on the persons, on the activity, or on the persons who perform the activity? The focus needs to be on the people who perform the activity. If the attention is only on the activity, the person becomes disposable. From this perspective, if a person is not accomplishing their duty, then another person is put in their place. This is how private companies function, within a mechanical view of life, although many are already reviewing this type of concept as they realize the substitution of people does not work. Many Spiritist Centers follows this system, giving importance to the activity, so that if the activity is not carried out correctly, the person is taken away and another one is put in their place. The focus is on the effect and not the cause.

When the focus is only on the person, as John has done, a process of make believe is created, where people are protected, based on pseudo-virtues that are mistaken for true virtues.

When the focus is on the people performing the activities, people are promoted as the immortal spirits that they are. How is a person promoted? Is each person allowed to do what they want, whenever they want? No! Each person, in serving, is invited to practice their conscientious duty, within the responsibility related to their task, accomplishing it in the best way possible, while at the same time undertaking actions of inner transformation, developing virtues of the heart.

Therefore, when a president acts with passive collaboration and negligence, he will not be engaged in the task of leading to accomplish the *strengthening of the weak*. As the spiritual Mentor said, a leader has to help those who still have not understood the great responsibility that is the work in the Jesus's field, and must help them to learn to regret their negligence, and to address the need to correct their mistakes and repair whatever damage they have caused.

Another important leadership responsibility highlighted in the text is the *sustaining of the strong*, in other words, those who are carrying out good works, encouraging them to persevere in their noble efforts. This is not accomplished through acts of excessive praise but, rather, by naturally motivating the good worker.

When will you stop taking notice of the small speck in your brother's or sister's eye, and instead, pay attention to the plank in your own? This plank is what blinds you and causes you to move from one failure to another. Believe what we, your spiritual kindred, are telling you. Every man and woman, proud enough to think of him- or herself as superior in virtue and merit to their brothers and sisters, is foolish and will be held accountable by Divine Justice.

A president of a Spiritist Center who believes him or herself to be superior to others and reprimands a worker who has made a mistake by belittling them, is acting with a lack of charity. The process is not of repression for the one who has erred, but of **sustaining** the one who still makes mistakes so that they can notice their errors, learn from them and try to repair them. All of us are in the same condition of learners of Life. When we judge, we are in conflict with the Law of Love, Justice and Charity in our own conscience, and we will suffer the consequence of this act.

In its true character, compassion is always modest and mild. It doesn't dwell on a person's defects but strives to rouse better qualities. The human heart may still be a pit of passions, but hidden in its innermost recesses are the seeds of good, the life force of the spirit.

This paragraph is also very significant. The commitment of a leader, as a president of a Spiritist Center, is that of motivating those who are led to perfect themselves.

In one dialogue the leader should, firstly, value the positive aspects of the other person, especially, their propensity towards goodness, because if there isn't any, then the person would not be involved in volunteer work. After this initial stimulus, a focus should be made on what is lacking, making sure to separate the person from their attitude. For example, as a volunteer worker in the Spiritist Center, he is very valuable, but his attitude of being absent without warning is unacceptable for the difficulties this causes etc.

We should never judge and condemn those who make mistakes, since by doing so we will be lacking in charity and indulgence. The correct action is to always offer help so that the person can resolve the problems that are created by their mistakes.

The Spiritist Doctrine is a source of blessings and comfort. Those who know it and who benefit from the uplifting teachings that are delivered from God's messengers, are indeed happy. For them, the pathway is illuminated. Along it, they can read the signposts that point them to the final goal of the journey. The signs call for putting love into action, for loving with all one's heart, for loving others like self. In short, we should extend unconditional love to everyone, and to God above all, for in our love for God we find a synthesis of all our responsibilities as human beings. For this reason, the practice of love is God's supreme Law.

This paragraph sums it all up. We will only act with Christian authenticity, charity, indulgence, tolerance and patience when we integrate and support all virtues in an active manner as we have reflected in these three chapters.

SELF–REFLECTIVE EVALUATION

- Close your eyes and connect with your inner self, exploring the content studied.

- Analyze yourself with authenticity, avoiding self-deceit.

- From the content, what did you understand that applies to your life?

- Has the content studied changed the way that you feel about the Divine Laws in yourself? If so, what changed?

- In this meeting we reflected on what is true charity and indulgence. Connect with your inner self, making an effort to feel the virtues in yourself. How do you feel? Form a more profound understanding of the Divine Laws in volunteer work and in the development of the essential virtues, as an axiom of these Laws. Did you notice an amplification of your own will to develop these virtues? How do you feel about this whole process?

- In this meeting, we have also reflected on how we should behave in interpersonal relationships in Spiritist Institutions. How have you evaluated your relationships? Are they in tune with the Christian purpose?

- What is it like for you to make efforts to apply all the Divine Laws in the activities of your volunteer work? How do you feel during this process?

- How do you feel about your life when applying the content studied? Do you feel that they it can change your life for the better, in a search for self-transformation and in your activities of carrying out good deeds?

- Now, recognize yourself as the immortal Spirit you are, who brings within the divine purview the determination to evolve until reaching relative perfection, through the pure understanding of the fulfilment of the Divine Laws, through the practice of virtues and by striving to be one with God. Submerge yourself profoundly into this spiritual truth. Feel and see yourself fulfilling the Divine Laws and developing all the essential virtues of Life throughout time, feeling the loving presence of God in your life.

- Gradually, start returning to a state of alertness. Open your eyes and write down your reflections.

7th Meeting

The Divine Law and volunteer work

part IV

Objective – To reflect on the meaning of the Divine Laws in our lives, in order to love, respect and apply them to volunteer work.

Initial refection – *Meditating on the meaning of the Divine Laws in our lives.*

- Close your eyes and connect with your inner self, in search of feeling as an immortal Spirit, a child of God, created to evolve and achieve plenitude.

- How do you feel?

- Have you surrendered yourself fully to God and His Laws?

• How have you dealt with the Divine Laws in your
volunteer work activities? Have you been applying them?

• Let your thoughts and feelings flow, avoiding any masks
or self-deceit. Be true to yourself, analyzing yourself with
authenticity.

• Now, open your eyes, returning to a state of vigilance.
Write down your experience; the feelings that you had,
the thoughts that came to mind, the sensations that you
benefited from.

REFLECTIONS BASED ON SPIRITISM
QUESTIONS FOR SELF-REFLECTION

• Knowing that the Divine Laws are present in our
conscience and that they exist for us to reach pure and
eternal happiness, what actions can we accomplish to love
and fulfill them in our volunteering activities?

• What are the practical means that can be used to manifest
the divine attributes and develop the essential virtues of
Life in volunteering activities?

In this meeting, we will continue to study the application of
the Divine Laws in volunteer work activities.

How to accomplish a volunteering activity in a Spiritist institution, within a christian proposal
part III

In past meetings, we studied the case of the president and
volunteer workers of the Spiritist Center. We will continue to study
the same case to point out other facets of it.

Before we start, we suggest that you re-read the case, which was narrated in chapter 4, to refresh it in your mind.

We will start our reflections with a text from *The Gospel according to Spiritism*, chapter IX, item 6, Obedience and Resignation, Lazarus, Paris 1863.

> Jesus constantly teaches fortitude and obedience to the Law, two virtues that go alongside gentleness and mildness of character. Unfortunately, many have mistaken such teaching to be the negation of will and self-determination. In fact, obedience is the consent of your reason; resignation, the consent of your heart. Both are active forces; both help shoulder the burdens necessary to your purification. Often those who are short of them, give themselves up to anger and quit their obligations. Indeed, the cowardly person can no more have fortitude than the proud and selfish can accept the Law. By contrast, Jesus was the very personification of obedience and fortitude, qualities which were much despised by society. He came to earth at a time when the dissolution of values had started to corrode Roman society, and He came to show to a dispirited human culture the benefits of renouncing an overly materialistic, self-centered life.
>
> Every stage of social development is identified by a dominant quality that propels it forward or a vice that restraints its progress. The quality of this current generation is its intellectual activity, its vice is its moral indifference. More than the sporadic insights of a few geniuses whose discoveries are well ahead of their times, intellectual activity refers here to the concerted efforts of society in general toward a goal possibly less dazzling, but more typical of the intellectual elevation of the era. Surrender then to the forward impetus that is given to your souls. Embrace the great Law of Progress, which is the motto of your generation. As for those who are either too complacent or aren't open to new understanding, they are the unfortunate ones. Sooner or later, their attitude will be changed by those who inspire the progress of humanity; their rebelliousness will be checked by means of the double action of brake and spur, when necessary. Eventually,

their resistance will wear out. In the meantime those who are mild and gentle will be blessed, because they are more receptive to new teachings – Lazarus (Paris, 1863).

As we have studied, the pledge of the immortal Spirit is to fulfill the Divine Laws, developing the essential virtues. Two virtues are essential for a person who wishes to perform their volunteer work in an effective manner, they are – Obedience and Resignation.

When we are deeply involved in the existential meaning of working for a good cause in our lives, in other words, when we have an existential objective in the volunteer work we will make efforts to develop obedience, the consent of reason, and resignation, and the heart's consent. It's a conscientious process that enables us to work with self-awareness and not from a sense of obligation, obeying the alerting-voices of our conscience.

A conscientious person who is reincarnated to accomplish the good to the limit of their strength will never fail to fulfill an obligation without a justifiable reason; if they have no other choice they will always give advanced warning so that a substitute can be arranged. This is what is lacking in several workers in the Spiritist Center administered by John.

Many people do volunteer work not because they are naturally motivated by a desire to do good works for the good of others, but because they feel an anxiety of conscience. In this behavior of pseudo-conscience they assume a posture, consciously or subconsciously, of offering bribes to God, Jesus, the superior Spirits etc. They want to be protected from a possible obsessive influence; to be supported by the Mentors when they disincarnate; to cure themselves of some infirmity etc. and for this reason they assume responsibility for a task in the Spiritist Center, but as the work does not constitute a clear existential objective in their lives, they do not take on the work with the necessary seriousness, because there is *no consent of reason*, let alone the consent of the heart.

Lazarus says that Jesus was the greatest example of these two virtues, and this is why he invites us to do hard work and to renounce our selfish impulses. What would happen once we understood in spirit and truth Jesus' proposal and the freedom it grants us? We would be attracted by this proposal and begin to learn about the necessity of detaching ourselves from the futile matters of life and material aspects of a society centered on *moral indifference*, consequently freeing ourselves through the Truth produced by a conscientious renunciation, as taught by Lazarus. His guidelines were communicated in 1863, but they continue to be very present, especially in these times of futility and superficiality.

To consciously renounce materialistic behaviors is to opt responsibly in favor of our own spiritual evolution. In Jesus' time and in the era of primordial Christianity, this virtue was profoundly understood and practiced in its most altruistic conception, to the point where people surrendered their lives for the love of Jesus, as did Peter, John, Mary Magdalene and Paul of Tarsus.

After centuries of distortion of the sublime lessons of the Master, the real meaning of the word "renunciation" was transformed, in a certain way, so that this word today means a process of martyrdom, in which the needs of penitence are required, especially through the aggressive harm to the body.

Psychologically, to renounce means to position oneself in a decisive mode before a challenging situation. It's a reinforcement of the term **enunciate**, which means *to clarify an idea*. Renunciation, therefore, is a profoundly courageous proactive attitude that has as its finality a permanent edification of the essential virtues of the heart. For this reason, it's intimately linked to obedience and resignation.

That's why Jesus invites us to initiate the journey of conscious renunciation, disconnecting from a selfish and egocentric personality, which causes personalism. By doing such exercises we will be solidifying our process of individualization and thus getting closer and closer to Him.

Personalism, a term that comes from the Latin Persona, is a result of experiences in superficial relationships that we've had throughout successive reincarnations, cultivating moral indifference. Individualization in its turn, is the Spiritual Being in its authentic sublimation, which is that of an immortal Spirit.

When we exercise real renunciation, we transcend the realm of the 'appearing to be' and move into the reign of *Being*, functioning without masks or exterior influences, and become profoundly connected with the Essential Being that we are and with God in a process of expansion of the conscience.

It's essential to exercise detachment from a life that is purely material in order to live spiritually. That does not mean disregarding or abandoning worldly life but, rather, giving value to spiritual and permanent matters.

For this reason, it's necessary to renounce purely earthly matters, being in the world without being of the world. True Christian Spiritists will be different from others, not because of living alienated from the world, but for being more aware that the world is transitory and that the meaning of life is in being aware of the Divine Laws inherent within our being, thereby effectively becoming a learner of the great Master Jesus.

The value of conscious renunciation starts with willpower. Our will is the exercise of wanting, and it can be of two types: the wanting in the field of desire, and the wanting in the field of action.

The wanting in the field of desire often drives the person to act in an imprudent manner, initiating a process and not completing it, as happens with many who initiate a task of good deeds, but do not conclude it. Or by getting involved only because they have nothing more interesting to do as in the case studied.

These individuals are enthused by goodness, but are still incapable of truly renouncing themselves to be able to conclude the actions in goodness. Enthusiasm is arrested in the search for compensation and recompense, as we have already analyzed. There is the exterior act, but without a profound reflection on why one should practice virtues of renunciation. Without this reflection, the enthusiastic person gives up on the task before actually acquiring true spiritual values.

On the other hand, wanting, when based upon a mentality of taking action, causes the person to act in a responsible manner, initiating and concluding every task of good deeds, for the love of Jesus's proposal. The individual who behaves in this manner practices **responsible renunciation**, in which the person fills themselves with enthusiasm for the activities to be fulfilled until concluding them.

In **responsible renunciation**, the person has as a focus on everything that it will develop in his or her heart. It's a decision that will build up the values of love, while knowing how valuable it is to choose humbleness instead of vanity, fraternity instead of pride, forgiveness instead of resentment etc., so that they can facilitate their individualization, as a faithful disciple of Jesus. The moral strength of the great souls of Humanity, admired by all of us, was only possible because renunciation was practiced, after a period of reflection, in a decisive manner.

This is the essence of conscious renunciation, one of the necessary virtues of individualization, in which the ego will gradually be transformed into the energies of the Essential Being. The ego exists to serve the Essential Being and not to remain battling with the Divine Essence in us. The process of inner transformation will never emerge from an inner battle, but from an inner pacification. This will only come about in the moment that we embrace our feelings as apprentices of Life, and learn to renounce the things of the world that are purely egoic, transitory in themselves, and actively promote the edification of the Kingdom of God within ourselves.

Renunciation, in light of this revelation, should not be interpreted as a disregard for everything that is of the world, or as a lack of interest in the things of life, according to what we have seen above. On the contrary, it should be seen as one of the most profound virtues, as it offers to "renouncers" the superior force of faith, courage and plenitude.

It isn't, therefore, an escape from the reality of the world, but an essential search for plenitude in the direction of the essential question of life. It's a decision that will lead us to being and will help us to overcome the need to appear to *be*. Renunciation is a virtue par excellence, which invites us to disseminate love not only through our intentions, but also through our conduct. And this is the very condition that is necessary to make oneself a sincere and true disciple of Jesus.

In the beginning of the twenty-first century the world is filled with unprecedented intellectual activities, producers of intellectualism and technological immersions. Moral indifference has also reached a level never seen before. It's clear that this also affects the Spiritist movement, in which many people feel inhibited in the development of their potential. People affected by these inhibitions, who would have had a great potential for producing fruitful work, end up doing very little, if anything, often times acting in a lukewarm manner, without enthusiasm.

Spiritism is based upon free will, and does not forces us to do anything. Consequently, the Spiritist movement also follows the same principle. This is why many volunteers who work in the Spiritist movement confuse liberty with libertinage, wanting to act without any discipline and obedience to Spiritist principles.

For this reason, it's essential to exercise virtues, especially with regard to the duty of conscience, along with renunciation, discipline, obedience and resignation, making us conscious workers, in keeping with Lazarus's exhortation: *Embrace the great Law of Progress, which is the motto of your generation. As for those who are either too complacent or aren't open to new understanding, they are the unfortunate ones.*

So that we can connect with the duty of conscience, accomplishing good deeds to the limit of our forces, it's imperative to free ourselves from moral laziness, by means of the Laws of Progress and Labor, practicing the virtues studied.

Many people complain that they do not know how to develop virtues. We will study the following self-reflective dialogue offered by the Spirit Honório, by the means of the mediumistic spoken instruction received by the medium Afro Stefanini II, so that we can surrender ourselves to the Divine Laws, developing virtues.

Our commentaries will be shown in italics.

Example: reflection on how to develop the virtue of discernment. This method also serves to develop any other virtue.

We will develop discernment within our heart. Discernment requires the observance of one Law, as a seed wants the contact with air, water and the sun in order to germinate and flourish.

The sun represents God, the air represents the Laws, and the water is the relation between the divine attributes and the Laws, as Divine Foresight and Providence are manifested.

Providence is the solicitude, the care God has for all of us. The Divine Foresight is the presence of the Divine Laws in our conscience.

I want to become a person capable of discerning the difference between that which I can and should do, and that which I can but should not do. In order for this process to begin, before anything else, there is a Law I am invited to respect. What Law would that be?

The Law of Progress.

Consequently, the Law of Progress, which is a Law that is profoundly connected to other Laws, invites us to practice another Law. What Law is that?

The Law of Labor.

The Law of Progress, in conjunction with the Law of Labor, mobilizes the will power so that there may be continued, patient, perseverant and disciplined efforts to develop discernment or any other virtue. Why is this necessary? It is so because no one progresses from one minute to the next without laboring.

It's the urge to progress that drives the human beings to utilize their will power to develop virtues, as in the case of the person who is unsatisfied with the way in which they are living and decides to be better. This choice, the exercise of the Law of Freedom, is driven by the Law of Progress, since it's one of the unstoppable divine determinations that we will achieve pure happiness, as proclaimed in the answer to question 115 of *The Spirits' Book*. There is a constant inflow from God to all His creatures, inviting them to evolve.

As the popular saying goes, there is no progress without work. This no not only valid only for material matters, but also, and above all, for the existential matters of Being. Virtues will not be developed simply because we wish them to be, but through effective work in developing them.

When looking to develop ourselves, we will notice that it is only possible through following the Law of Labor. From then onwards we will be feeling the presence of another Law. Which one?

The Law of Cause and Effect becomes evident, because we will be feeling the beneficial effects of our efforts to change through the practice of discernment.

We can now notice the Divine Laws beginning to add up to one another, just like virtues do. As the spiritual Benefactor says in the dialogue, the Law of Labor, in unison with that of Progress, stimulates the will power, and invites us to develop some critical virtues which will help in the development of other virtues later on. These critical virtues are: continued effort, patience, perseverance and discipline. From this effort (cause), which is accomplished by the exercise of self-love (another virtue), we will be feeling the benefits of our efforts (effects), strengthening us in the practice of virtues.

Many still believe that the Law of Cause and Effect is a law God created to punish people. It's thought that it's linked only to the ill use of free will and its consequences. However, as is the case with all other Divine Laws, this Law exists so that we can evolve.

We are stimulated even more to progress when we feel the immediate effects of our own efforts to become virtuous. These actions make our lives more subtle and gentle, as taught by the Master Jesus. It's the Law of Cause and Effect that provides this, since, if the cause is good, the effects also will be. In the same way, if the cause is moral laziness, the effects will be of pain and suffering. It's the whip and spur that Lazarus speaks of in the texts studied above. This is why it's important to develop virtues of discernment so that we may make better choices.

Whatever the virtue may be, when we make an effort to exercise it we will feel the effects of well-being, inner joy, a feeling of belonging to the Universe, because we will be connected to our will power and the Divine Will, fully feeling the inflow of God stimulating us toward progress.

When we start to feel the Law of Cause and Effect, if we listen

*to our hearts, we will feel the effects of the virtue of discernment. Out of
the joy of conquering this virtue, we begin to feel another Law. Which
Law is it?*

The Law of Love!

*And because we are filled with the Law of Love, we want other
people to have the same feeling. This causes which Law to emerge?*

*The Law of Charity, which invites us to do unto others that which
we would like them to do unto us.*

*When we promote the Law of Charity, we feel profoundly just,
and enter into contact with the Law of Justice. The path continues as we
want to do more and more, practicing more virtues and so on.*

In this moment we activate another Law. Which Law is this?

*At this point, having engaged in virtuous practice, we surrender
profoundly to the Law of Gratitude, becoming truly grateful.*

To evolve means to fulfill the mission given by God to all
of us. It's intimately linked to the Greater Law of Justice, Love and
Charity. The actions we take, in order to develop virtues while fulfilling the Divine Laws, are just, loving and charitable towards ourselves and others.

In order for us to navigate the path towards the practice of
virtues with the necessary precision, it's necessary to ask ourselves
if the actions we are about to take are loving, fair and charitable towards ourselves and others. If the answer is yes, we can proceed because we will most certainly be connected to the divine within ourselves. But if the answer is no, we should make an effort to change
our choices. In cases where we have doubt, we need to invert the
process and ask: if what I want to do was done to me, would I like it?

We notice that in our dialogue, the Mentor Honório offers
us a didactic resource. In our daily practice there is no way of separating the Laws, nor the virtues. We are invited to notice that in

certain moments we focus more on one Law or one virtue, and that our efforts can be made gradually and continuously, with patience, perseverance and discipline. One virtue associates with one another, which nurtures the previous, and this creates a *virtuous* cycle.

Is there a more self-loving attitude than that of developing a virtue which will make our lives more harmonious? Obviously there isn't, and that is why, when we make such efforts, we will end up living in a state of gratitude. A person starts to live with so much inner joy that all that remains is gratitude towards the Creator for the blessings that stimulated the conquest of virtues, by one giving oneself fully to the fulfillment of the Divine Laws.

> *This is the meaning of the Divine Laws in our lives, which is directly related to the presence of these Laws in our conscience and with our profound act of surrendering to them, which is expressed by the development of virtues within ourselves.*
>
> *The Divine Laws, can be compared to the margins of a river, comprised of the vegetation surrounding it, etc., and the virtues are the waters of the river.*
>
> *The same process utilized to develop discernment can be used to develop all other virtues.*
>
> *In this exact moment the Supreme Intelligence of the Universe, the Primary Cause of all things, is working without interruption for our happiness. Let's reflect upon this, that the most powerful Being of the Universe, the Supreme Heart is, in this instant, using all of the energies of His Supreme Will to see us completely blissful.*
>
> *It is the Divine Providence and Foresight constantly guiding us to the supreme encounter with the Creator. If otherwise, where would be the omniscience, omnipotence and omnipresence of the Creator be?*
>
> *To benefit from all of this, it is necessary to take actions to surrender to the Laws of God is necessary.*

Honório

Self-reflective evaluation

- Close your eyes and connect with your inner self, exploring the content studied in this meeting.

- Analyze yourself in an authentic manner, avoiding self-deceit.

- From the content, what did you understand that applies in your life?

- Did the content studied change the way you feel the Divine Laws in yourself? If so, what changed?

- In this meeting we reflected on the virtues of obedience, resignation and renunciation, which are essential to accomplishing a volunteering activity in a harmonious manner. Connect with your inner self, making an effort to feel the virtues within. How do you feel? Proceeding from a more profound understanding of the meaning of the Divine Laws in the volunteer work and benefiting from the development of the essential virtues as in the practice of these Laws, has there been an amplification of your desire to strengthen these virtues? How does this process feel for you?

- In this meeting we reflected on a method to develop virtues. How do you evaluate this method? Do you feel it can be used in your life?

- What is it like for you to make this effort of fulfilling the Divine Laws in your volunteer work activities? What is it like for you to carry out these efforts to you?

- How do you feel about your life in applying the content studied? Do you feel that it can improve your life in your search for self-transformation and in your activities in the practice of good deeds?

- Now, recognize yourself as the immortal Spirit you are, who brings within the divine purview the determination to evolve until reaching relative perfection, through the pure understanding of the fulfilment of the Divine Laws, through the practice of virtues and by striving to be one with God. Submerge yourself profoundly into this spiritual truth. Feel and see yourself fulfilling the Divine Laws and developing all the essential virtues of Life throughout time, feeling the loving presence of God in your life.

- Gradually, start returning to a state of alertness. Open your eyes and write down your reflections.

8th Meeting

The Divine Laws and family relationships

part I

Objective – To reflect on the meaning of the Divine Laws in our lives, in order to love, respect and apply them within the family environment.

Initial reflection – *Meditating on the meaning of the Divine Laws in our family relationships.*

- Close your eyes and connect with your inner self, in search of feeling as an immortal Spirit, a child of God, created to evolve and achieve plenitude.

- How do you feel?

- Have you surrendered yourself fully to God and His Laws?

- How have you dealt with the Divine Laws in your family relationships? Have you been applying them?

- Let your thoughts and feelings flow, avoiding any masks that contribute to a process of self-deceit. Be true to yourself, analyzing yourself with authenticity.

- Now open your eyes, returning to a state of awareness. Write down your experience; the feeling you had and the thoughts that came to mind, the sensations that you benefited from.

REFLECTIONS BASED ON SPIRITISM
QUESTIONS FOR SELF-REFLECTION

- Knowing that the Divine Laws are present in our conscience and that they exist in order for us to reach eternal happiness, what actions can we accomplish to love and fulfill them in our family relationships?

- What are the practical means that can be used to manifest the divine attributes and develop the essential virtues of Life in family relationships?

In this meeting we will study the application of the Divine Laws in the family, specifically within conjugal relationships.

The Divine Laws and conjugal relationships

We will study the situation of a relatively common family. This is a true story, but the names and several specific details have been modified so as to protect the identity of individuals.

Andrew and Cindy were a young couple with three children, nine-year-old Carlos, five-year-old Eduardo and Debora, a three-year-old. Andrew is a dedicated Spiritist and Cindy has difficulty in understanding her husband's dedication. She is tied to worldly matters, as she really enjoys going to bars, clubs and parties in general. Every once in a while, Cindy falls into depression, isolating herself in her room due to feeling bored with her life, even thinking of committing suicide.

Although Andrew does not feel comfortable in those kinds of places his wife likes going to, he usually accompanies her to avoid conflict and to be able to spend time with her outside of their household because she does not accompany him to Spiritist activities and demands his presence at the parties and bars she goes to.

Andrew believes he is responsible for guiding his wife towards a more spiritual life, since he intuitively feels that he has misguided her in a past live. For that reason, he gives in to her wishes in an effort to maintain a peaceful marriage and, in his way of thinking, to be able to guide his wife towards a more spiritual way of life as time goes by.

However, Andrew does not feel satisfied with the situation, since for him it's a sacrifice to go to the places his wife enjoys. Nevertheless, he believes that if he stops going, his wife will end up leaving him.

Although he sees the harm this routine causes, even to their children, as often times his wife returns home drunk and he himself, against his beliefs, ends up drinking to accompany her, he continues with the same behavior.

As Andrew sees it, even though he loves his children very much, these years of marriage have been the worst of his life. His wife provokes him daily, wanting to fight. Often times they get into huge arguments, only stopping just short of physical aggression.

On other occasions he behaves passively, accommodating himself to the situation so as not to make his children suffer even more.

When he has a serious fight with his wife, Andrew thinks about getting separated in order to put an end to the torture his life has become, but he feels guilty for thinking this way and imagines what life without him would be like for his children, living with such a mother.

Although he remains faithful to his wife in spite of this tumultuous relationship, Andrew feels very lonely and often times thinks of having extra-conjugal affairs.

Let's reflect on the case of Andrew and Cindy, illuminated under the light of the triad: immortal Spirit, Divine Laws and God, using the content of the Spiritist Codification and of the Gospel of Jesus.

When there is turmoil in the conjugal relationship, as in the case of Andrew and Cindy, the relationship between parents and children, will also be in turmoil. Avoiding any judgement of the couple, we can evaluate the situation, with the objective of learning from what is happening with them, and attempt to discover what can be done to overcome these conflicts.

Remembering that the triad of immortal Spirit, Divine Laws and God, invites us to embrace surrender and actions, we can surrender ourselves to God and the practice of the Divine Laws, acting through the immortal Spirit, and developing the essential virtues of life.

In analyzing the difficulties of the couple with regard to this triad, what are the main problems experienced by Andrew and Cindy? They struggle with surrendering to the Laws of God, and exercising virtues.

Surrender and action constitute in an inseparable duo. There cannot be surrender without action and there cannot be action without surrender. We should surrender to God proactively, maintaining His attributes in us. We surrender to the Divine Laws, developing the corresponding virtues.

Limitations of Andrew in relation to divine attributes

As far as the divine attributes go, Andrew manifests the following limitations:

Attribute: Unicity

Limitation: Personalism and Dehumanization

Andrew nurtures the personalism of a good guy, like the Professor Joseph, and John, the president of the Spiritist Center, from the cases previously studied. When he is a *good guy* with his wife, doing everything she wants, even though his behavior is contrary to his beliefs and values, he assumes a posture of personalism.

He mistakenly bases his actions in a common psychological game played in interpersonal relationships, taking upon himself the role of martyr-savior for his wife and children. He martyrizes himself to "save" the family members. He believes that he has the responsibility of saving his wife from herself, and saving the children from their mother's negligence.

The dehumanizing aspect dehumanization comes about when he argues with his wife, becomes indifferent to the difficulties in their marriage and thinks of having extra-conjugal affairs. But these reactions are soon suffocated because his strongest psychological behavior is personalism, always thinking of being a "good" husband and a "good" father, the savior of the family.

The best course of action for Andrew would be to follow his conscience and develop his individualization, working effectively to fulfill the Divine Laws already known by him, developing virtues he is lacking.

Attribute: Supreme Benevolence and Justice
Limitation: Cruelty, Pseudo-benevolence, Injustice and Pseudo-justice

Andrew demonstrates cruelty without realizing it, because it's hidden within his personalism, the generator of pseudo-benevolence. When accompanying his wife to her parties, and drinking alcoholic beverages, he does harm to himself because, although knowing and feeling that he should behave differently, he ends up doing what she wants. He practices pseudo-benevolence with his wife. However, in truth, he is injecting cruelty into their lives.

Other times, when they fight almost to the point of physical aggression, cruelty appears in a more explicit manner. During these verbal aggressions, exchanges of toxic energies take place, totally poisoning their home, and negatively affecting themselves and their children.

Although these actions may seem fair at times, when there is personalism these actions are in truth, profoundly unfair towards all involved.

Because Andrew practices pseudo-benevolence, he is directed toward passive collaboration through his own omission. This behavior brings about harm in the day to day living with his wife. When he neglects to live the truth, developing virtues, he creates evil for himself and the whole family.

Personalism masquarades as reality and makes us choose the easier path of living a life of false values, instead of one where benevolence and justice are developed. These are virtues requiring hard labor to be achieved, which is perfectly possible when one is willing to make continuous, patient, perseverant and disciplined efforts.

Attribute: Immutability

Limitation: Pseudo-inalterability and Volubility

Andrew fosters pseudo-inalterability and volubility at the same time. By exercising personalism he concentrates his energies on seeming, instead of being. He wants to remain in "good graces" with his wife, by passively collaborating with her desires. He practices a permissive behavior and maintaining a dubious attitude with a focus on the masks of the ego. When the mask of "good husband" no longer sustains itself, he becomes aggressive, showing the evidence of the conflicts he maintains within.

Andrew believes that the problem is not with him, but with this woman who does not want to develop herself spiritually. He projects onto his wife his volatile behavior, which prevents him from making efforts to develop virtues, working towards his own individualization and essential immutability. He thinks he is giving the best of himself, without realizing that it's necessary to go beyond the way in which he is behaving.

Attribute: Omnipotence

Limitation: Impotence, Pseudo-omnipotence and Despotism

Andrew fosters pseudo-omnipotence when he believes he has the power to save his wife and children. He thinks that he is all-powerful. However, when he realizes that his behavior is not correct, he begins to exercise despotism, arguing aggressively with his wife, only to fall, soon after, into the impotence of passivity and apathy. He remains in this vicious cycle between pseudo-omnipotence, despotism and impotence, distancing himself from the potency, or in other words, from the actions that would allow him to accomplish self-transformation by means of the practice of the Divine Laws and the exercise of virtues.

Only by becoming a virtuous person can Andrew can become a better husband and father, and to motivate his wife and children to do the same. The virtue development exercise explained in the previous chapter can be applied here.

Attribute: Omniscience
Limitation: No Conscience and Pseudo-conscience

Andrew oscillates between no conscience and pseudo-conscience. When acting contrary to the knowledge he possesses of the reality of life he becomes inconsequent, exerting cruelty and volubility. Other times, he applies a pseudo-conscience behavior, acting as a pseudo-wise person, because of his personalism. That takes place because he misconstrues Spiritist precepts, of which he does not yet have a deep understanding, and upon which he is still unable to reflect as to how they pertain to his life. Because of this lack of understanding he thinks that he can be the savior of others, which indicates a blunt disrespect for the Divine Laws.

He should study and learn in detail the science behind Spiritist precepts, reflecting profoundly upon them in his life so that these precepts can make a positive difference in his family's day to day life.

This is why it's not enough to have the intellectual knowledge of the Truth, as Andrew has. It's necessary to bring the Truth within ourselves, by reflecting upon the knowledge we are gaining and on what certain concepts represent in our lives. Only by reflecting in this way will we be able to feel these concepts in our hearts, internalizing them and living in accordance with the Truth.

When we connect profoundly with the truth, we free ourselves, according to Jesus' teachings in John, 8:32 – *Know the truth and the truth shall set you free.*

Attribute: Eternity
Limitation: Post-occupation and preoccupation

In Andrew's case, mistaken behaviors of post-occupation and preoccupation constantly take place.

He preoccupies himself intensely with the spiritual salvation of his wife and the future of his children, to the point of becoming anxious and embracing a personalist posture, putting on egoic masks, and trying in vain to live the lives of the family members for themselves.

The post-occupation emerges when Andrew thinks of freeing himself from the burden he has imposed upon himself, and then experiences feelings of guilt for having thought of separating, or for having lamented that all those years of marriage have been the worst in his life.

When we are invited to manifest the eternity of God, our objective is to concentrate on the present, on the here and now. Time is made through a succession of present moments. When we post-occupy by lamenting over something or blaming ourselves, we distance ourselves from the objective of being present in the now, because of our focus on the past. When we preoccupy ourselves, we are trying to anticipate the future. As the popular saying goes, the future belongs to God. Hence, the reason why both post-occupation and preoccupation behaviors cause turmoil within us becomes clear.

Andrew should make efforts to concentrate on the present, accomplishing what is within his reach, which is learning from his own mistakes, doing the best he can to repair them while at the same time making efforts to accomplish self-transformation, as an immortal Spirit, child of God and apprentice of Life. Moreover, he should also work on educating his children in the practice of virtues.

Attribute: Immateriality
Limitation: Pseudo-spiritualism

Andrew acts in a pseudo-spiritualist manner because he does not use the academic knowledge he already has of Spiritism in his life, and in his day to day living in the family realm.

Because he already possesses intellectual knowledge of the Truth, Andrew has a duty of conscience to make efforts to reflect upon Spiritist teachings, especially on the meaning of the Divine Laws in his life and to find ways to integrate their meaning into his feelings. In this manner he will become capable of meaningful interactions, so he can truly live as an immortal Spirit. This is the only way for knowledge to become felt and lived, consequently making a positive difference in interactions with his family.

Attribute: Presence
Limitation: Isolation

When Andrew feels impotent in relation to his omnipotent objective of changing his wife, he isolates himself in essence because he does not make an effort to exercise his real power, developing virtues to feel the presence of God in his life and in the life of his loved ones.

Because of pseudo-omnipotence, which is a competition with God, he begins to exercise impotence and isolates himself from the divine within, consequently also isolating away God, even putting himself in a position to have feelings of abandonment.

In this moment Andrew remains unmotivated and thinks of giving up on his marriage, but soon returns to the posture of pseudo-omnipotence, which is his strongest behavior.

It's important to reflect that God never isolates Himself from us and never abandons us. We are the ones who isolate ourselves from the divine essence that we are, and consequently from God. However, as God is omnipotent, His constant influx of love towards us encourages us to reconnect with God sooner or later.

Limitations of Cindy in relation to divine attributes

Further on we will study the limitations Cindy manifests in relation to the divine attributes:

Attribute: Unicity
Limitation: Dehumanization

Cindy manifests dehumanization in an intense manner. For example, when she becomes inebriated, and disregards her responsibilities as a mother, whose main task is to support her children in their efforts to connect with God, she behaves in a very dehumanizing manner.

Imagine how inhumane it is for small children to be forced to observe their mother in a drunken state. Cindy does this and doesn't even care.

Unfortunately, this behavior is very common in a materialistic, hedonistic and superficial society, which believes that a human being has (materialistically speaking) the right to make the most of life, doing exactly what Cindy does: nights out at parties and clubs, drinking etc. Any behavior that causes harm to us or to others is inhumane.

When behaving in such a manner, a human being is in truth, dehumanizing, because the person is distancing him or herself from individualization, in other words, from the efforts of becoming each time a better person through the practice of virtues.

Attribute: Supreme Benevolence and Justice
Limitation: Cruelty and Injustice

By acting in an inhumane manner, Cindy fosters cruelty and injustice, even though, in relation to her children for example, although she does not have the intention of treating them badly or unjustly, Regardless, that is exactly what she ends up doing.

Cindy behaves with clear cruelty and injustice towards her husband, although Andrew is not actually living an injustice, since he is atoning for the mistakes made toward her in the past. However, the fact that he is atoning does not exempt Cindy from being responsible for the harm and injustices she has committed.

Attribute: Immutability
Limitation: Volubility

Cindy distances herself from the commitments as a mother and spouse to experience purely egoic pleasures. She behaves like a typically shallow person, in other words, like one who is egoistically satisfied without being concerned with what happens to others around her. As we have already said, a mother has a very significant commitment towards her children, which is that of bringing them closer to God. How can a mother do this if she herself has become distanced from God? Behaving like this, Cindy distances herself from her conscientious duty, thus assuming serious debts before her own conscience.

Attribute: Omnipotence
Limitation: Impotence and Despotism

Cindy oscillates between prepotency and impotence. It's the typical case of subtle obsession. Her personality oscillates between a process of exaltation and a process of inhibition of the personality. This is caused by the emotional imbalance within herself, which is worsened by the bad spiritual influences.

When she loses her cool, she behaves as a despot toward her husband and her children. At other times she inhibits herself, feeling impotence because she cannot do or make her life be the way she wishes it would be, and for this reason she becomes depressed. This happens mainly due to the exacerbated rebelliousness and pride that she harbors.

Impotence takes hold when she isolates herself, locking herself up in her room in a process of depression.

Attribute: Omniscience
Limitation: Lack of Conscience and Pseudoscience
The actions of Cindy are profoundly disconnected from her conscientious duties. It's a very serious behavior pattern because it places at risk the psycho-emotional and physical integrity of her children, as she refuses to enlighten herself with the Truth.

Attribute: Immateriality
Limitation: Materialism
All of Cindy's actions are driven toward hedonism and materialism. Everything that makes people distance themselves from achieving individuation is materialistic. However, many people don't even notice their strong attachment to material things, often times even continuing to participate in their religious activities, as did Cindy.

Attribute: Presence
Limitation: Isolation and Annihilation
Because of the way Cindy behaves, she isolates herself in essence, putting herself into a deep state of depression. While feeling depressed, she thinks of killing herself to be free from the suffering of which she has been the main cause of, in a clear attitude of annihilation.

Many people kill their own body because they believe that life in the body is the cause of their suffering, and for that reason they try to annihilate themselves through suicide, because they ignore the fact that suffering is caused by their spiritual rebelliousness and that they will continue to live, suffering even more until they become tired of suffering and decide to submit to the Divine Laws, working towards individualization.

Now, we'll reflect upon how this couple can improve their conjugal relationship.

The path towards a healthy relationship is the fulfillment of the Divine Laws through the development of the essential virtues of Life and manifestation of the divine attributes.

So that Andrew can develop virtues, as Life is inviting him to do so, he must realize that he bears more responsibility for the success of the relationship, because he has a broader level of understanding of life than his wife does.

Only through exercising his reason, reflecting upon and feeling the reality of the conjugal relationship, transforming it into a challenge-experience, used to obtain several learning-experiences through the development of virtues, will Andrew will be able to triumph in the relationship instead of acting in a personalist manner as he has been doing.

For this, it's necessary that Andrew sees the marriage from the point of view of the Divine Laws, as a process of voluntary choice to practice the Conscientious Duty by practicing the Law of Love, Justice and Charity. This is the way in which he can truly help Cindy to see the world from another angle, as well as to develop the harmony that is necessary to become a better father to his children.

In the next meeting we will reflect upon the concept of marriage and what results can be achieved in it through the practice of the Law of Love through the exercise of the virtue of love.

SELF-REFLECTIVE EVALUATION

- Close your eyes and connect with your inner self, exploring the content studied in this meeting.

- Analyze yourself in an authentic manner, avoiding self-deceit.

- From the content studied, what do you think applies to your life?

- Has the content studied changed the way you feel about the Divine Laws in yourself? If so, what changed?

- In this meeting, we reflected upon the conjugal relationship as a challenge-experience so that the couple can fulfill the Divine Laws, developing virtues. Connect with your inner self, making an effort to feel your marriage in this manner, if you are married. If you are not, reflect on the meaning of the fulfillment of the Divine Laws and development of virtues.

- How does your life feels when applying the content studied? Do you feel that it can change your life for the better in your search for self-transformation and acts of good deeds?

- Now, recognize yourself as the immortal Spirit you are, who brings within the divine purview the determination to evolve until reaching relative perfection, through the pure understanding of the fulfilment of the Divine Laws, through the practice of virtues and by striving to be one with God. Submerge yourself profoundly into this spiritual truth. Feel and see yourself fulfilling the Divine Laws and developing all the essential virtues of Life throughout time, feeling the loving presence of God in your life.

- Gradually, start returning to a state of alertness. Open your eyes and write down your reflections.

9th Meeting

The Divine Laws and family relationships

part II

Objective – To reflect on the meaning of the Divine Laws in our lives, in order to love, respect and apply them within the family realm.

Initial reflection – *Meditating on the meaning of the Divine Laws in our family relationships.*

- Close your eyes and connect with your inner self, in search of feeling as an immortal Spirit, a child of God, created to evolve and achieve plenitude.

- How do you feel?

- Have you surrendered yourself fully to God and His Laws?

- How have you dealt with the Divine Laws in your family relationships? Have you been applying them?

- Let your thoughts and feelings flow, avoiding all masks, and excluding any process of self-deceit. Be true to yourself, analyzing yourself with authenticity.

- Now open your eyes, returning to a state of awareness. Write down your experience, the feeling that you had, the thoughts that came to mind, the sensations that you benefited from.

REFLECTIONS BASED ON SPIRITISM
QUESTIONS FOR SELF-REFLECTION

- Knowing that the Divine Laws are present in our conscience, and that they exist so that we can reach pure and eternal happiness, what actions can we carry out to love and fulfill them in a conjugal relationship?

- What are the practical means that we can use to manifest the divine attributes and develop the essential virtues of life in conjugal relationships?

In this meeting we will continue to study the application of the Divine Laws in family relationships, specifically in those that are conjugal.

The Divine Laws and the conjugal relationship

In the last meeting we began studying the case of the couple Andrew and Cindy. In this meeting we will analyze Spiritist principles that can serve as guidance in our own efforts to achieve a marriage that is based in the Divine Laws. Before we enter upon this endeavor, we suggest that you re-read the case narrated in the previous chapter.

According to what we have seen in Spiritist works, a healthy marriage results from the practice of the Law of Love through the exercise of the virtue of love as in the examples below:

Starting with *The Spirits' Book*:

Question 695. *Is marriage – that is to say, the permanent union of two people – contrary to the law of nature?*

"It represents a more evolved stage in human development."

Question 696. *What effect would the abolition of marriage have on human society?*

"It would mean a return to the life of the animals."

In the natural state, the union of the sexes is random and entails no responsibility. Marriage is one of the first signs that a social structure has developed. While conditions vary, marriage can be found among all peoples, establishing a principle of cooperation and mutual commitment between partners. The abolition of marriage would, we can be certain, return humanity to its infancy and would even place us below certain animals whose instinct lead to a lifetime bond to a single partner.

These two questions clearly demonstrate what marriage is for society. Nowadays there is an attempt to redefine marriage, making this relationship superficial, under the pretext of becoming more modern.

As Allan Kardec comments, any attempt to abolish marriage or to loosen the conjugal ties, as has been advocated, would place the human being below certain animals, birds and mammals, which unite monogamously their entire lives.

Question 697. *Is the idea that a marriage cannot be dissolved found in the law of nature, or is it a human law?*

"A human law, altogether contrary to the law of nature. But

humans change their laws at will. Only natural laws are unchangeable."

Marriage is in conformity with Natural and Divine Laws, however its indissolubility is contrary to these Laws. Let's study the reason why from a text *of The Gospel According to Spiritism* chapter XXII, items 2, 3 and 4:

Everything human is subject to change. The only unchanging things are those that emanate directly from God. Thus, while the laws of nature are the same at all times and in all countries, human laws vary according to times, places, and intellectual progress. What is of a divine order in marriage is the union of the sexes, so that the replenishment of the population might be sustained. But the conditions that regulate this union are so human in their makeup that in the whole world, even the Christian part of it, there are no two countries where the laws governing unions are exactly the same and where, over time, these laws don't undergo amendment. What it legitimate according to the civil laws of one country during one particular time may very well constitute adultery in another country and at another time. This is because the civil law aims at regulating individual interests that can vary considerably depending on local customs and requirements. For example, in some countries only religious marriages are recognized; in others, a civil marriage is required as well; in others, a civil marriage by itself is sufficient.

Now, along with the natural law pertaining to the physical union of the sexes and reproduction, which is of a divine order and applicable to all living beings, there is another divine law, equally unchanging but pertaining chiefly to the moral realm: the law of love. Providence wants human beings to unite not only through the ties of the flesh, but those of the soul. In this way the mutual caring and affection between a husband and wife can be passed on to their children, as lessons in love. Together the two of them, not just one, are expected to love and care for their children and help them progress. One might wonder, however, whether it is genuinely the law of love that shapes the lives of most ordinary couples. In many cases the answer is No. All too often, what sustains the marriage is not the mutual affection that binds one to the other – those feelings have long been shattered. What then are these couples really looking for in marriage? Rather than the joys of the heart, many see it as a way of furthering their own egos, of ostentation, of satisfying their greed, and other purely material interests. As long as these interests are well served, the marriage suits them well. Well-lined pockets, people say, make any match a good one, for they are supposed to assure the couple's happiness. Yet neither civil laws nor the obligations these place on marriage partners can replace the law of love. If a marriage is not governed by love it will fall apart no matter how binding the marriage contract. Where the vows taken at the altar are simply recited as an empty formula, they make a sham of matrimony. Here we have the seeds of dysfunctional marriages, and sometimes of tragic ends, a double disgrace couples could avoid if, in their lives together, they didn't neglect the one condition that gives divine sanction to their union: the law of love. When God said, "And the two will become one flesh," and Jesus added, "Therefore, what God has joined together, let man not separate," we should understand their words as referring to marriages consummated according to God's unchanging Law and not according to human laws, which are changing in nature.

Do we really need the civil law then? Should we go back to marriage as it existed in the state of nature? Certainly not. The purpose of civil law is to regulate social relationships and family interests in such a way that the two coincide with the requirements of society. The civil law is both useful and necessary, varying though it often is. It must also be farsighted because today's human beings cannot live like their primitive predecessors. Further, there is nothing – absolutely nothing – that prevents us from shaping the civil codes to reflect the Divine Laws. It is only the stubbornness of misconceived notions of social interest that impede the enactment of laws inspired by the Divine Code. Fortunately, the hold of these laws is waning and a more illuminated understanding is emerging. Such notions will disappear completely with moral progress, which will open humanity's eyes to many wrongs, including the failings and even crimes that come from marriages based solely on material interests. One day society will ask if it's really more humane, more charitable, more ethical to chain together people who can't live with each other than it is to give them their freedom, and whether marriages that can't be ended don't actually increase the number of adulterous relationships.

When reflecting upon the relationship between Andrew and Cindy from the perspective shown in the text above, we can see that marriage is in accordance with the Natural and Divine Law and that the impossibility of its dissolution is contrary to the same Law, making us conclude that marriage should be a relationship guided by the Law of Love and that it should initiate and remain voluntary during the whole life of the couple.

In reading the story of the life of this couple, we noticed that both of them feel obligated to remain in the marriage, especially Andrew, but, in spite of the desire to separate, they continue to remain married and maintain a relationship full of conflict.

There are reasons for this, according to what we have recently analyzed, but for now we will reflect on Allan Kardec's insights, which originate in what the superior Spirits teach us about marriage.

In our society, the myth of a romantic love is sought after within marriage, the type found in fairy tales, in which marriage is enacted so that the couple can live happily ever after. Many couples, questing after love in an infantile manner, look for this happiness through marriage without reflecting on the real meaning of the Law of Love.

On our planet Earth, many marriages are a process of atonement, as in the case of Andrew and Cindy, who were drawn to one another due to the Law of Attraction, which determines that the indebted feels attracted to the one to whom the debt is owed and vice versa, but at the same time, they repel one another by not observing the Law of Love as the basis of their union.

In marriages of atonement, the exercise of the virtue of love, in order to apply the Law of Love will be a real challenge. On the other hand, the process is different in trial marriages, in which couples have already been attracted by a positive affinity they have built in their spiritual past. This factor will make it easier for them to build a loving relationship. In marriages of atonement, the abuses of the past towards one another are like heavy chains that should be transmuted through the exercise of love.

In order to successfully overcome this process of atonement, love should be exercised to alleviate the pain and to atone, meaning, to extract the inner purity, transmuting the impurities of past abuses by exercising the Law of Love, Justice and Charity.

As seen in the story of the couple, Andrew as the one who is indebted, is the one who has the greatest ability to exercise the Law of Love, by being a role model to Cindy and the children.

Let us analyze the behavior of Andrew based on the triad expressed in figure 4, which may be found in chapter 2, to determine how he should act:

- Recognizing that he is distancing himself from the attributes of God – Andrew distances himself from several attributes, especially that of the one of individualization, often times believing that he is behaving correctly, by behaving like a savior to his wife and children. Because of this behavior he also ends up practicing personalism and various other egoic behaviors already analyzed in the previous chapter.

- Recognizing that he is not fulfilling the Divine Laws, instead of believing to be fulfilling them.

- Recognizing that he is developing pseudo-virtues instead of the essential virtues of life.

- Recognizing that it's not his responsibility to save his wife and children, but to motivate them to self-renewal as the loving Existential Beings they are.

Before we continue reflecting on virtues that Andrew has as a conscientious commitment to develop, we will analyze two basic questions in the history of his life:

- When Andrew thinks of separating, he feels guilty because of what could happen to the children and also because of the feeling that he is indebted to his wife because of their spiritual past.

- He also thinks of having extramarital relationships in order to gain affection.

As we have seen above, the conjugal relationship is voluntary, since there is nothing in the Divine Law nor in the civil law, more specifically in our country, that obligates someone to remain married. Some questions though, should be taken into consideration, so that every relationship can be self-healing, and so that those involved don't feel they are being forced to be in it, which would not be helpful to their spiritual growth.

To purely and simply get separated while still consciously feeling a commitment to a marriage, even if the marriage is in the midst of a painful process, is something that should only be carried out in exceptional cases, as we will see further ahead.

Let us now study parts of two messages from the Spirit Lazarus, extracted from *The Gospel According to Spiritism*.

Chapter XI, item 8, The Law of Love:

Love sums up the complete doctrine of Jesus, for it is the most sublime human sentiment.

Sentiments themselves are a result of the transformation of instincts as human progress follows its course. At the very beginning of evolution, humans had only instincts. In the next stage they became capable of sensations. Finally, with more intellectual progress and greater spiritual refinement, humans reached a level at which they were capable of genuine emotions. Now, as we have said, the finest and highest emotion is love – not love in the common sense of the word (that is, romantic love), but love as an inner sun that, at its burning center, concentrates the soul's highest aspirations and its essential divinity. The law of love substitutes for individualism the reconnection of all beings. It eliminates social ills. Consequently, those who transcend their physical nature and come to love wholeheartedly all who face suffering, are blessed. Indeed, they are blessed, for their love of others makes their own spiritual and physical challenges appear trivial. Their step is light and they live as if they were outside and beyond themselves. This is why, when Jesus pronounced the divine word "love," the ancient world trembled and the martyrs, enraptured with new hope, walked fearlessly to meet death in the Roman circus.

[...]

We have said already that, at the beginning, human beings were predominantly governed by their instincts. Therefore, if your character is dominated by instincts, you remain closer to the starting point than to the goal. Reaching this goal requires that you transcend the instincts, bringing to light your more noble thoughts and feelings. You can perfect the latter by overcoming your tendency to live only for the material world.

In many of your instincts you will also find the seeds of higher feelings. Instincts bring with them the drive toward progress; they are like the acorn that hides within itself a great oak tree.

Individuals dominated by their passions, then, are in earlier stages of evolvement. They change very reluctantly, and only slowly come out of their shell. The spirit, you must understand, needs to be cultivated as you would cultivate a pasture. All your spiritual wealth in the future depends on the work of cultivation you are doing now. More than any of your material achievements, this is the work that will take you to glorious heights. As you come to understand the law of love, you will begin to experience the sweet delights of the soul. These delights are preludes to your heavenly happiness. – Lazarus (Paris, 1862).

When reflecting on the teachings of Lazarus in the context of marriage, we can observe that: At the very beginning of evolution, humans had only instincts. In the next stage they became capable of sensations. Finally, with more intellectual progress and greater spiritual refinement, humans reached a level at which they were capable of genuine emotions. The evolution of human beings should happen in an ascendant verticality of life. Although Andrew has conscientious impulses to evolve vertically, he still desires to satisfy his instincts and sensations, and ends up focusing on personalism, a behavior based on pseudo-love. In this motion of repressing his egoic desires, he thinks he is a virtuous person, which he is not, because he is only repressing his negative feelings instead of freeing himself from them by developing a sentiment of love, or purifying himself as explained by Lazarus.

The Mentor says: *The law of love substitutes for individualism the reconnection of all beings.* Only through the exercise of the Law of Love, can personalism be overcome and the process of individualization flourish, by transforming one's personality in order to live as an immortal Spirit temporarily incarnated. Thus the affirmative: *Now, as we have said, the finest and highest emotion is love – not love in the common sense of the word (that is, romantic love), but love as an inner sun that, at its burning center, concentrates the soul's highest aspirations and its essential divinity.*

Lazarus says that love exists in the vulgar sense of the term. What does he mean by that? It's the romantic love of fairy tales, which does not require an effort to develop, and happens at first sight. In truth, this feeling isn't love, it's passion, that constitutes in an irrational fire, a perishable madness.

As we have studied in chapter seven, there are Laws and their corresponding virtues. Lazarus, in his message elaborates on both, placing the virtue of love as this "inner sun" that brings us closer to our immortal form through the means of individualization, as we develop all the virtues derived from love. Thus the assertion of Lazarus: *Reaching this goal requires that you transcend the instincts, bringing to light your more noble thoughts and feelings. You can perfect the latter by overcoming your tendency to live only for the material world.*

It's what Andrew is invited to develop according to Lazarus's recommendation: *The spirit, you must understand, needs to be cultivated as you would cultivate a pasture. All your spiritual wealth in the future depends on the work of cultivation you are doing now. More than any of your material achievements, this is the work that will take you to glorious heights. As you come to understand the law of love, you will begin to experience the sweet delights of the soul. These delights are preludes to your heavenly happiness.*

So that the Spirit can search for his individualization, becoming more spiritual, it's essential to embrace two other Divine Laws, the Law of Progress and of Labor. Nobody progresses without work. Often times couples want to have a harmonious marriage without actually putting any effort into it that would help to make the relationship become more affectionate as time goes on.

The Law of Love, existent in our conscience waits for the exercise of the sentiment of love. The Law already exists and all that remains is to attune to it through the practice of the virtue.

If we expect the other to practice a virtue, we will remain passively waiting without working on our inner self, so that we can in the first place change ourselves. That's how Andrew mistakenly behaves. What does he want? He wants his wife to become a loving spouse, changing the way she treats him. After all, he is doing everything he can to save her from herself, and he waits for Cindy to change transforming into an affectionate wife.

Love begins in the process of the one who loves giving instead of wanting to receive, in a way that the giving party can experience the *sweet delights of the soul,* as Lazarus teaches.

Andrew acts in a passively supporting manner towards his wife, doing as she wishes, in a pseudo-love behavior, so that she will give him affection.

However, as this proposal is false in itself, disregard is received in return.

Therefore, if a marriage is searched for with this objective in mind, there isn't in fact a real union; there is a paper signed or a religious ceremony, but there is no relationship. So that there may be a conjugal relationship, the practice of the Law of Love and the sentiment of love need to be observed.

The Law of Duty must be observed so this wish of a loving marriage can be achieved. We will give further study to another message of Lazarus in the same context of marriage, focusing on the couple Andrew and Cindy.

The Gospel According to Spiritism, chapter XVII, item 7:
Duty is a moral obligation, first to the self and then to others. Duty is a fundamental law of life. It is expressed in the smallest and in the most elevated human actions.
[...]
As such, duty is, in essence, a matter of free will. The conscience acts as the guardian of virtue as well as its caretaker, but frequently it is powerless against the deceptions of desire.

Here Lazarus says that the conscientious duty is a moral obligation of our Being. Firstly with ourselves and then towards others. It's what Andrew must focus on to free himself from a salvationist personalism, because by behaving this way he gives in to the sophism of passion, living a fallacy, believing that he has a duty to save his wife and at the same time his children from her negative influence.

Andrew is, constantly, invited to practice the consciential duty of repaying his debt before life, according to notion that – *The conscience acts as the guardian of virtue.* However, because of this personalist behavior, the inclinations to run away from his conscience is very strong, by means of engagement in extra-marital relationships in order to have the affection that is missing, as he tries, simultaneously, to deceive the appeals of his own conscience. When he actually take the time to reflect upon his behavior, he feels guilty, and falls into a vicious cycle that runs from escaping the calling of his conscience, to the a feeling of guilt, and back again.

Where does this feeling Andrew has of being responsible for the misdirection of Cindy comes from, including the present need to redeem her, which is a feeling he distorts by transforming it into a game of salvation? Let's search for the answer in *The Spirits' Book*:

> Question 392. *Why can't the incarnate spirit remember its past?*
> "As human beings you cannot, and may not, know everything. God, being wise, has determined so. Without the veil that hides certain things from you, you would be dazzled, as if you had suddenly passed from darkness to light. Through the forgetfulness of the past, you are more fully your essential selfs."

> Question 393. *"How can we be held responsible for our deeds, and rid ourselves of our faults, if we do not remember them? How can we gain by experiences acquired in lives we have forgotten? We might understand that the trials of life are a lesson to us if we could only recall the wrongs that have brought those trials about. But if we forget our former lives, each new life must be like the first one, so that all the work must begin again. How can we reconcile this with God's justice?*

"With each new life a spirit becomes more discerning and more capable of distinguishing between good and bad. What would happen to free choice, however, if the spirit remembered all its past? When a spirit re-enters its original life (that is, the spirit-life), its whole past unrolls before it, revealing the faults it committed, the causes of its sufferings, and what it could have done to prevent those faults. It then understands the justice of the situation it is in and seeks out a new life that will help it repair the mistakes of the life it has just left. It asks for a new trial similar to the one in which it failed or which it considers likely to aid its progress. And its requests that its superiors in the spirit-world help it to succeed in the new trial. It knows that the spirit who will guide it in the new life will give it an intuition of its past faults and so assist in curing them. These intuitions come like a natural, deeply felt desire to resist certain impulses. You may attribute your resistance to the teaching you have received from your parents, but it is in reality the voice of your conscience. It is an echo of your past, warning you not to fall back into the faults of your previous lives. The person who undergoes the trials of the incarnate life with fortitude and resists its temptations consequently rises in the hierarchy of spirits when he or she returns to the spirit-world."

While we don't have an exact memory of what we have been and done in the past, we do have, during our present incarnate life, an intuition of our previous lives. This intuition takes the form both of instinctive tendencies and conscience. In other words, the intuition of the past gives rise to an intent to avoid committing the same mistakes again.

These questions talk about the Law of Forgetfulness. Why did God create this Law? It's a Law created to protect us from ourselves. Our reason tells us that the consequences of remembering the mistakes we've committed in the past would be horrific. What if Andrew could remember the cruelties he imposed on Cindy in a past life, such as, hypothetically speaking, a situation in which he had used her sexually and abandoned her afterwards, causing her to end up in a brothel as a result? And what if she remembered having been victimized by him? Would they be able to get married now? Of course not, because their memories would bring about many intense feelings of remorse, resentment, hatred and other egoic sentiments toward each other.

But as we have seen, this forgetfulness is never complete, since we have an intuition of the commitments we accepted before we reincarnated, of which our Spiritual Guide and our own conscience, constantly reminds us. Andrew feels this calling of his conscience, which is why although he desires to commit adultery and abandon his marriage he does not do it so. But the reason why he does not do it so, is because he is repressing his feelings, because of the guilty he feels. The correct set of mind would be to harmoniously accept the calling of his conscience to fulfill the spiritual commitments he previously embraced.

An extra-marital relationship in search of affection is, in truth, a sophism that Andrew creates to deceive his own conscience, which is why he feels even greater guilt when thinking of this possibility.

Life invites him to be faithful by the practicing the virtue of the duty of conscience, the practice itself having been made possible by choosing to strive mightily to hear the voice of the conscience, following the Laws of Freedom and Responsibility, and transforming once and for all the criminal desire of adultery and abandonment, acts already committed by him in a past life, for which he has the duty of creating a new meaning in this new chance of redemption.

As the spiritual Benefactor explained, when a Spirit resists temptation, it elevates itself and ascends in the hierarchy of the Spirits, upon returning to their midst.

This is only possible by faithfully fulfilling the Law of Labor, which is accomplished by daily, continuous efforts, marked by patience, perseverance and disciplined so that the feeling of love may be developed. But what is to become of Andrew's desire to have a loving wife, living happily within the relationship? If he is faithful he will be able to have such a marriage in this way in a future reincarnation, after he has repaired his faults by following the Law of Love.

What he can have now is the relative happiness of a well fulfilled duty.

SELF-REFLECTIVE EVALUATION

- Close your eyes and connect with your inner self, exploring the content studied in this meeting.

- Analyze yourself in an authentic manner, avoiding self-deceit.

- From the content studied, what did you understand that applies in your life?

- Has the content changed the way you feel the Divine Laws within yourself? If so what changed?

- In this meeting, we reflected upon the conjugal relationship as a challenging experience so that provides couples with an opportunity to fulfill the Divine Laws, especially the Laws of Love, Duty, Progress and of Labor, developing virtues in the conjugal relationship and in the family in general. Connect with your inner self, making an effort to feel your marriage in this way, if you are in a marriage. If not, reflect upon the meaning of fulfilling the Divine Laws and developing virtues in the family relationships as a whole.

- Connect with your inner self, making an effort to feel love. How do you feel it? Starting from the understanding of the Divine Laws in family relationships and in the development of the essential virtues as a proxy of these Laws, has there been an amplification of your will to develop these virtues? What is this like for you?

- How do you feel your life in applying the content studied? Do you feel that it can improve your life as you strive for self-transformation through acts of good deeds?

- Now, recognize yourself as the immortal Spirit you are, who brings within the divine purview the determination to evolve until reaching relative perfection, through the pure understanding of the fulfilment of the Divine Laws, through the practice of virtues and by striving to be one with God. Submerge yourself profoundly into this spiritual truth. Feel and see yourself fulfilling the Divine Laws and developing all the essential virtues of Life throughout time, feeling the loving presence of God in your life.

- Gradually, start returning to a state of alertness. Open your eyes and write down your reflections.

10th Meeting

The Divine Law and family relationships

part III

Objective – To reflect on the meaning of the Divine Laws in our lives, in order to love, respect and apply them within the family.

Initial reflection – *Meditating on the meaning of the Divine Laws in family relationships.*

- Close your eyes and connect with your inner self, in search of feeling as an immortal Spirit, a child of God, created to evolve and achieve plenitude.

- How do you feel?

- Have you surrendered yourself fully to God and His Laws?

- How have you been working with the Divine Laws in your family relationships? Have you been applying them?

- Let your thoughts and feelings flow, avoiding masks, and turning away from self-deceit. Be true to yourself, analyzing yourself with authenticity.

- Now open your eyes, returning to a state of awareness. Write down your experience: the feeling that you had, the thoughts that came to mind, the sensations you benefited from.

REFLECTIONS BASED ON SPIRITISM
QUESTIONS FOR SELF–REFLECTION

- Knowing that the Divine Laws are present in our conscience and that they exist for us to achieve pure and eternal happiness, what actions can be taken in order to love and fulfill them in a conjugal relationship?

- What is the practical means we can use to manifest divine attributes and develop the essential virtues of life in conjugal relationships?

In this meeting we will continue to study the application of the Divine Laws in family relationships, specifically within marriage.

The Divine Laws and conjugal relationships

In the previous meetings we studied the case of the couple Andrew and Cindy. In this meeting we will continue to analyze Spiritist principles that serve as guidance for us to follow and be able to achieve a marriage that is based on the Divine Laws. Before we initiate, we suggest that you re-read the case narrated in chapter 8.

As we saw in the previous meeting, a true and loving relationship does not come readily to anyone, as is thought by those who believe in romantic and easy love found in fairy tales; instead, it's gradually constructed by the couple's daily efforts, performing many exercises in this challenging experience called marriage.

This is why in a marriage, especially the atoning type experienced by Andrew and Cindy, and by extension, any marriage marked by trials, it's possible to deal with the relationship in three ways:

- **GREATER EVIL** – Make the marriage a chronic illness, during many years. The relationship is extremely toxic, resulting in physical and emotional illnesses for both partners, and the children in cases where children are present. This is the way Andrew and Cindy have lived their relationship, making it a great evil, because they do not attempt to exercise the Law of Love, he, by fulfilling his duty of conscience with humbleness and resignation, and she by forgiving him for what took place in the past, so their relationship can be renewed.

- **LESSER EVIL** – To legally separate, ending a marriage that, in truth, no longer exists. This measure will prevent years of unnecessary resentment and suffering. In this case, the couple will take advantage of a situation where at least a minimum level of friendship still exists between them, especially when they have children and look to maintain a harmonious paternal and maternal relationship. They minimize resentment and hurtfulness, avoiding the greater evil. It's like an amputation of a member that has gangrene in order to preserve the life of the person, analogous to saving the sanity of the couple. Many couples who avoid separation fall into the category of greater evil instead of developing the greater good.

As we have concluded previously, from our study of the observations of Allan Kardec in *The Gospel According to Spiritism*, marriages, except when motivated by ulterior interests or spiritual immaturity, do not happen by chance. This is the reason why, when there is a separation in an atoning or trial type of relationship, the experience of atonement or trial is then delayed, but that is still preferable than to maintaining a toxic relationship that can end up causing greater evils, such as suicide and murder as is often seen.

- **GREATER GOOD** – since the marriage is a voluntary relationship, the mature decision would be to transform the relationship into a greater good, an effort that can be made by at least one of the involved parties in order to achieve a healthy relationship. This is only possible with great effort towards the fulfillment of the Divine Laws and the practice of virtues.

So that there may be a greater good, it's necessary to question oneself: *Since I have decided to maintain my conjugal relationship, what actions can I take in order to make it better and healthier?*

By not working effectively in this direction, one becomes susceptible to failing into the greater evil. As we have already concluded in our studies, the practice of the Law of Love, and the virtues of Love, is only possible through the continuous application of patience, perseverance and disciplined exercises.

The ideal is that both spouses are willing to develop the greater good, but this is not always possible, as in the case studied. Because Andrew is a person who has more knowledge of the spiritual truths, he is the one who is most responsible for maintaining the greater good, even if Cindy remains on the sidelines.

So that the greater good may be developed, two essential areas must be invested in: the interpersonal and relational. Certain specific virtues must be worked on in each of these areas. Let's study them.

In the interpersonal area, the first step Andrew can take to live in a healthy manner is to work on his affection for himself, because he will not derive the desired affection from his present atoning marriage. Self-affection will connect him with the duty of conscience and with the Greater Law of Love, Justice and Charity.

When Andrew desires affection in the conjugal relationship, and due to the lack of such, he thinks of reaching out to extra-conjugal relationships, he transfers to another person, that which he should be searching for within himself.

We are talking about very profound conscientious matters, linked to the Divine Laws present in our conscience, and not what is usually advocated in the superficial and hedonistic society of the present day. Currently "happiness" is sought after in a selfish and egocentric manner, as if we could achieve in a superficial manner something that is internal and profound. No one can truly be happy by running away from a duty of conscience.

Self-affection is the result of a loving and self-embracing exercise that, in its turn, is the consequence of the practice of five essential virtues:

◇ **Self-esteem** – as the children of God that we are, we bring within ourselves the same potential as that of pure Spirits. To practice self-embracing in a loving manner, we must engage in exercises to feel ourselves as immortal Spirits, children of God, and apprentices of Life, thus developing self-esteem. Self-love is essential to mobilizing the will to change and to transforming us into Conscientious Beings.

◇ **Self-acceptance** – meaning an unconditional acceptance of ourselves as students of Life, who bring many limitations to be transformed, and who will evolve by making right choices, but also through making mistakes. All of us have potentials and limitations. Our potentials should be developed to overcome our limitations, utilizing of course, the best of our present abilities. There will only be self-acceptance if we are willing to accomplish these exercises with humbleness and with full recognition of the deficiencies we have, while making efforts to gradually overcome them. Only by reflecting upon these truths will we be able to accept that we carry egoic feelings in need of transformation, instead of continuing to use psychological masks to deceive ourselves.

◇ **Self-confidence** – relates to having unconditional confidence in the possibilities of overcoming our limitations, seeing all our experiences as blessings of life, invitations for us to develop *learning-experiences*, developing our capacity of self-transformation. We must trust our ability to behave righteously, while nevertheless, conceding the possibility of making mistakes. By exercising confidence in Life and in God, and by making ourselves better and more self-aware individuals, despite our many limitations, we have the full potential to overcome them.

◇ **Self-value** – is the act of valuing ourselves as we are, with our limitations, possibilities and potentials, instead of thinking we are worth what we do, what we have or what we pretend to be. We must attribute to ourselves our real value as children of God, Spirits in evolution, students of Life and heirs of the Universe, created for happiness.

◇ **Self-respect** – meaning to respect ourselves as human beings in evolution, while also respecting others, placing limits on the relationships we have with other people so we can also in return be respected.

The exercise of these five virtues will depend solely on the efforts of the individual person, and are imperative to bring about an emotional balance that can be utilized in the development of virtues that are necessary for the task of perfecting a marriage.

Let's see in practicality how Andrew could have behaved in a loving self-embracing manner. As an example, in moments when his wife provoked him by questioning him about something or saying something negative about him, because Andrew did not exercise self-embracing, what did he do instead? He retaliated against his wife's provocations immediately, arguing aggressively with her.

By exercising self-embracing in a loving manner, he will learn to practice *proactive silence*, in other words, he will become silent when suffering aggression, exercising the precept taught by the Master in Matthew, 5:39 – *But I tell you, do not resist an evil person. If someone strikes you on the right cheek, turn to him the other also.*

The most common behaviors people have in these cases are either to retaliate or to egoically silence themselves. The first instance is an aggression, which is contrary to the *turn the other cheek* teaching, is based on the law of Talion, an eye for an eye, a tooth for a tooth. The egoic silence is when the person does not actually say anything but mentally keeps on thinking about the aggression received, and energetically retaliates against the aggressor, while presenting a seemingly peaceful exterior for all the world to see. It's a personalist behavior of pseudo-inalterability, focused on the seeming instead of the being. In these two behaviors, toxic energies are exchanged and cause harm to all the members of the family.

How does *proactive silence* work? It's the silence of the mouth outwards and from the mouth inwards, in which the person will exercise the five virtues studied so that there may be harmony in the interpersonal relationship with the aggressor. Since the person is exercising self-embracing with love, this is possible. By practicing the Law of Love, Justice and Charity towards oneself first, the person will then be able to behave the same way towards others.

It's the practice of the Christian teaching *"do unto others as you would have them do unto you"*, in the most practical manner possible, understanding that if we were the ones having and unhappy and aggressive moment, we would be thankful if others were to practice *proactive silence* towards us.

Many have said that this is very challenging. Yes, that is true. It's easier to retaliate that it is to exercise Christian virtues, but it's essential that we inspire ourselves in our Model and Guide, the master Jesus, in order that we may become better people, exercising the duty of conscience and accomplishing what is good to the limit of our strength, as we have learned in all the cases studied in this book.

As he begins to practice self-embracing in a loving manner, Andrew can gradually transform his marital relationship into one that is healthy, even if Cindy continues to behave irresponsibly. The development of five essential virtues makes this a possibility, as one finds affinity with the duty of conscience and lovingly self-embraces: **unconditional love, renunciation, compassion, meekness** and **humbleness** are necessary to make the marriage a truly challenging transformational experience.

- **Unconditional love** – is the virtue resulting from the practice of the Law of Love, Justice and Charity, a must to achieve harmony in any intra-relationship or inter-relationship.

This is the love that does not impose anything onto the ones who are being loved. It is the *inner sun,* as the Spirit Lazarus says in the message already studied, which needs to be exercised daily and without restrictions.

As an example, if a spouse pierces the other with a *needle*, the *cotton* of unconditional love will used as protection from the needle, as many times as it may be necessary. This degree of love is only possible when one begins at the starting point of actively exercising self-embracing.

Is it fair? The dimension of justice in the greater Law advocates that we have the right to be blissfully happy. However, one does not benefit from such a right without the practice of a duty, and this only happens through the practice of virtues. Unconditional love is the guiding compass during our travels in the pursuit of happiness.

Is it charitable? If Andrew behaved within the spectrum of these five virtues he would be doing to Cindy that which he would like to have done to himself. If in the past he acted in an unloving, unfair and uncharitable manner towards Cindy, his best option at this present time would be reparation by offering *the other cheek*.

- **Renunciation** – is the result of spiritual maturity, as it drives a person to overcome the desire to have the ideal partner as a spouse. Such a partner, who always understands us and always makes us happy. Such a person does not in fact exist. It remains only in the imagination of those who are still tied to the infantile myth of marriages that can make us happy without the necessity of putting any hard work into it.

In real life all of us have qualities and imperfections and it's necessary to renounce the person we idealize in our minds so we can learn to live with a real person, mutually helping each other to overcome our imperfections and to practice virtues.

- **Compassion** – from the moment we begin to develop renunciation, we feel a need to also develop compassion toward our spouse, who still carries, within him or herself, many limitations to be transformed.

Cindy deserves Andrew's compassion, because she is a person who is suffering greatly due to the manner in which she has chosen to face the challenges presented to her in the present life. She has an excess of repressed negative feelings that cause her to suffer, with much hurt and resentment, exacerbated by a decided lack of self-love, and requiring compassion on the part of her spouse, Andrew, who is already sufficiently spiritually developed to be in a condition to exercise this great virtue.

The practice of compassion will be imperative during the exercise of proactive silence, because during this silencing it's important that the person prays for the aggressor, visualizing light being transmitted from his or her heart towards the aggressor, exercising in an effective manner unconditional love, renunciation and compassion, offering the other cheek, and transmitting healthy energies to the spouse instead of developing toxic energies.

If Andrew behaves in this manner, not only will he benefit Cindy and their children, but also, and especially, himself, as he will be pacifying his own heart, and will have avoided intoxicating himself with his own negative energies of hatred added, which would have added to those coming from his wife.

- **Meekness** – is a virtue that invites us to accept others as they are, with both their qualities and their limitations. It's the mother of patience and tolerance, which in their turn are virtues that must be practiced in order to have a healthy marriage.

- **Humbleness** – is a virtue that gives meaning to the four previous virtues because it makes us recognize how little developed we are when it comes to spiritual evolution as well as pinpointing the imperfections we still have within us. In this process, we begin to be more loving and understanding towards others, tolerating their deficiencies, knowing that we also need others to be more loving and understanding towards us.

The exercise of these virtues brings about a virtuous cycle in which unconditional love feeds renunciation, which feeds compassion, which feeds meekness, which feeds humbleness, which in its turn brings about unconditional love.

By behaving in this virtuous manner, Andrew invites Cindy, in a loving way, to transform herself with his own example of change for the better, in the same way that he invited her to indulge in the vices of the past, only now his invitation is one of moral and intellectual development, accomplished by exhibiting continuous efforts of patience, perseverance and disciplined exertions to develop the duty of conscience.

Now, let's reflect upon Cindy's psychological behavior by analyzing a few aspects within her personality that life is inviting her to modify. No one reincarnates on Earth to remain stagnant in a position such as the one in which Cindy stubbornly chooses to stay in, without indebting themselves before their own conscience.

Based on the triad: Immortal Spirit, Divine Laws and God, here is how Cindy should behave:

- Recognizing that she is distancing herself from the attributes of God.

- Recognizing that she is not following the Divine Laws.

- Recognizing that she is immersing herself into an egoic behavior by developing egoic passions instead of essential virtues of life, which is the reason why she reincarnated again.

Basing our reflections on Allan Kardec's works, let's expand our understanding as to how Cindy should behave, using her case as an example for people who might identify more or less with her way of behaving.

We will start with a few questions from *The Spirits' Book*:

Question 132. *Why do spirits incarnate?*
"God has established incarnation as the means through which spirits eventually become perfect. Spirits themselves experience incarnation in different ways. For some, it is a process of purification; for others, it is an opportunity to fulfill a mission. Whatever the individual experience, however, reaching perfection requires that every spirit undergo the entire range of experiences particular to existence in a material form. The effectiveness of the purification process, in fact, resides in accumulating these experiences."

Question 117. *Are spirits themselves responsible for hastening their progress towards perfection?*
"Certainly. The length of time it takes them to reach their goal depends on their desire to do so and on their observance of the Law. After all, don't compliant children learn quicker than idle, stubborn ones?"

Cindy, although she has reincarnated in order to evolve through atonement, which is an action for the purpose of extracting the essential purity within oneself, chooses to rebel against submitting to the will of God, which is that all his children should follow the Divine Laws so that they may achieve spiritual plenitude and happiness. In so doing she increases her own suffering.

Cindy becomes fixated upon seeing herself as a victim, and ends up acting in a way that boycotts her happiness and consequently the happiness of her family, as she subconsciously tries to avenge herself against Andrew and, ultimately, against Life itself.

It's of utmost importance for her to begin a process of reflection and think about the negative impacts her actions are having on her spouse and children, and on herself, making everyone feel unhappy. This reflection should be followed for her own good, by a submission to the Sovereign Will of God.

Cindy should exercise her free will in the direction of listening to the voice of her conscience, because all children of God are under the influx of the Divine Will so that they may progress, but is necessary to connect our will power to the Supreme Will, as per to the teaching of A Protector Spirit in *The Gospel According to Spiritism*, chapter XIII, item 10:

> [...] Some of you will say, "Bosh! There are so many of us here on earth that God can't possibly see each one of us." Listen carefully, friends. When you are on the top of a mountain, don't you see the millions of grains of sand that cover it? This is the way God views you. Like the sand that is allowed to go where the wind blows, God allows you your free will so that you can do as you want. But there is a condition: God has put a vigilant spark in you called conscience. Listen to it because it will give you good advice. Sometimes, sad to say, you manage to numb it. You welcome into your life negative forces, and the conscience goes silent. But you can be certain as soon as you begin to have even a little regret, your rejected conscience will make itself heard. So listen to it, probe it, and you will be amazed by the uplifting guidance you will obtain.

God gave us the freedom to choose between good and evil. This is the reason why, in the process of the evolution of the immortal Spirit, there are always possibilities for opting between the two different paths: the submission to the good, or the lack of submission which directs us to behaving in evil or pseudo-good ways. Sooner or later, this lack of submission will have as a consequence, the *shadow of remorse*.

If Cindy decides not to change, she will feel intense remorse upon saying farewell to the masks of the superficial existence in which she is living. Normally, this happens after disincarnation. Very few stop to hear the voice of their conscience and correct themselves while they are still in the blessed physical existence.

Returning to *The Spirits' Book*:

Question 574. *What is the mission of the intentionally idle on Earth?*
"These people are to be pitied for their poor judgment. They will one day account for their time. Usually they start experiencing the results of their unwise lifestyle in this very life by the disgust and boredom they feel."

– Since these people were given a choice, why did they prefer a lifestyle that could benefit no one?
"Among spirits, just as among humans, there are some who reject a life of usefulness and work. God allows this happen, knowing that the spirits will eventually understand the burden of their uselessness and will be the first to ask for an opportunity to make up for lost time. It may also happen that a spirit chooses a more useful life but, once incarnate, strays from it under the influence of indolent beings. As a result, it feels incapable of being useful."

Cindy fits perfectly into the descriptions portrayed in the questions and answers above. Because of her moral laziness the most important work she should be concentrating on is her submission to the Divine Laws. Since she refrains from developing virtues she hasn't yet acquired, her duties as a mother, wife, citizen, and so on remain compromised. The result is that she feels such a dissatisfaction with her life that she even thinks of killing herself, although she is a mother of three children.

This entire disharmony is taking place because of her subconscious boycott of her own happiness. This unhappiness is being produced by her rebelliousness and moral laziness that often times are taken advantage of by avenging inferior Spirits who were, at one time or another in the past, harmed by her, Andrew or their children, as explained in question 574a by the spiritual Mentors. These Spirits utilize Cindy's and Andrew's negative spiritual tendencies to cause them more affliction, aggravating even more the spiritual situation of the family.

We will conclude these reflections with question 945 of *The Spirits' Book*:

> *What should we think of people who commit suicide because they are bored with of life?*
> "They are unfortunate but foolish. If they had used their time doing some useful work, life would not have been such a bore for them."

Because of her dissatisfaction with life, a dissatisfaction caused by her own rebelliousness and moral laziness, Cindy thinks of killing herself, so as to escape from dealing with the unhappiness she has caused to herself and her family. In line with materialistic thinking, despite the fact that she has some spiritual knowledge, she believes that taking the life of the body will end all her suffering. An ill-informed mistake!

What is very interesting is the answer of the spiritual Mentors when talking about work as a source of existential meaning. In that answer, the word *work* should be seen in the broader sense, not only as professional occupations and volunteer work, but above all, individual and transferable work to make efforts toward self-transformation.

This is the reason why moral laziness is so harmful. It impedes the main work that we are invited to accomplish which is the work of fulfilling the Divine Laws, and developing the essential virtues of life. By practicing moral laziness, the individual creates a paradox. By not taking action to change their lives, they expect to live an easy life, without work. However, this behavior causes a negative life transformation because inutility ends up making life very heavy, so heavy that the person then wishes to free herself from it by committing suicide.

For those who are willing to work actively to create their own well-being by helping others in every way possible, life will be laborious, but contrary to the consequences produced by moral laziness, they will experience a lightness of being instead of heaviness, because of their love and respect for the Divine Laws, especially of the Laws of Love, Justice and Charity, as Jesus wisely taught us: *For my yoke is easy and my burden is light.* (Matthew, 11:30.)

Self—reflective evaluation

- Close your eyes and connect with your inner self, exploring the content studied in this meeting

- Analyze yourself with authenticity, avoiding self-deceit.

- From the content studied, what did you understand that applies in your life?

- Did the content studied change the way in which you feel the Divine Laws in yourself? If so, what changes were these?

- In this meeting, we reflected on the conjugal relationship as a challenging experience, so that spouses can develop virtues that are real jewels, such as loving self-embracing and unconditional love, renunciation, compassion, meekness and humbleness in a marriage and in the family in general. Connect with your inner self and, if you are married, think about your actions within your marriage. If you are not married, reflect upon the meaning of fulfilling the Divine Laws and developing these virtues in your interpersonal relationships.

- Now, strive to feel the Law of Love and the virtue of love. How do you feel? Starting at a more profound understanding of the meaning of the Divine Laws in family relationships and the development of the essential virtues as an axis of these Laws, has there been an amplification of the desire to develop these virtues? How does this process feel for you?

- How do you feel about your life in applying the content studied? Do you feel that it can improve your life in the search for self-transformation and in activities of practicing good deeds?

- Now, recognize yourself as the immortal Spirit you are, who brings within the divine purview the determination to evolve until reaching relative perfection, through the pure understanding of the fulfilment of the Divine Laws, through the practice of virtues and by striving to be one with God. Submerge yourself profoundly into this spiritual truth. Feel and see yourself fulfilling the Divine Laws and developing all the essential virtues of Life throughout time, feeling the loving presence of God in your life.

- Gradually, start returning to a state of alertness. Open your eyes and write down your reflections.

11th Meeting

The Divine Laws and family relationships

part IV

Objective – To reflect on the meaning of the Divine Laws in our lives, in order to love, respect and apply them within the family realm.

Initial reflection – *Meditating on the meaning of the Divine Laws in our family relationships.*

- Close your eyes and connect with your inner self, in search of feeling as an immortal Spirit, a child of God, created to evolve and achieve plenitude.

- How do you feel?

- Have you surrendered yourself fully to God and His Laws?

- How have you dealt with the Divine Laws in your family relationships? Have you been applying them?

- Let your thoughts and feelings flow, avoid all masks, and excluding any process of self-deceit. Be true to yourself, analyzing yourself with authenticity.

- Now open your eyes, returning to a state of awareness. Write down your experience: the feeling that you had, the thoughts that came to mind, the sensations from which you benefited.

REFLECTIONS BASED ON SPIRITISM
QUESTIONS FOR SELF-REFLECTION

- Knowing that Divine Laws are present in our conscience and that they exist so that we can reach the pure and eternal happiness, what actions can we accomplish to love and fulfill them in parent-child relationships?

- What is a practical means that we can use to manifest the divine attributes and develop the essential virtues in Life and in the parent-child relationship?

In this meeting we will continue to study the application of the Divine Laws in family relationships, specifically in relation to parent-child relationships.

The Divine Laws and the parent-child relationship
part I

In this meeting we will work on the story of the family of Andrew and Cindy, focusing on their relationships with their three children.

The relationship between Andrew and Cindy, and its effect on the three children: Carlos who is nine years old, Eduardo, who is five, and Debora, who is three, are full of contradictions because the disturbed relationship of the couple dramatically impacts their parent-child relationships.

For Cindy, it is almost a form of torture to look after her children. When she is required to look after them, she complains profusely, saying that she was not born to be a nanny. Because of this mindset she tends to mistreat her children, shouting at them and being verbally aggressive, at times even being physically aggressive or showing indifference to their needs.

Andrew in his turn assumes the posture of an overly protective parent who tries to defend his children from their own mother, because of the inconsequent manner in which she deals with motherhood.

Andrew is an engineer and is always working, averaging 12 hours a day, including many weekends. He does that in order to give his children a comfortable life, taking care of their household expenses such as having a housekeeper, and a nanny, and he also covers costs related to the children's private school and extracurricular activities. Often times he feels guilty for working so much and leaving the children in the care of the nanny, but he says there is no other way.

Cindy sporadically engages in freelance work, but stays home most of the time. However, when she is at home she is never available to look after the children.

Another problem caused by Andrew is permissiveness, as he spoils his kids by satisfying all their wishes to compensate for their mother's indifference and his own absence. For example, when the children do not want to participate in the Gospel at home, Andrew does not say anything. Often times he lets the children make their own choices, even he knows their choices are bad for them, using the excuse that they need to exercise their free will.

In this troubled environment, the children grow up without learning about limits and boundaries that are so necessary for their education. Because of these spiritual problems, as well as vibratory and physical energy problems at home, Debora and Eduardo have many health issues. The conflicts between the brothers are constant, and this is also the case between the children and their mother. The spiritual interferences faced by the family are clearly seen, while the parents take no action to effectively resolve the current situation.

Let's analyze this family history based on the immortal Spirit, Divine Laws and God triad. As was the case in their conjugal relationships, Andrew and Cindy disobeyed several Divine Laws and distanced themselves from God in regards to their previously accepted commitment of being parents.

Let's observe figure 5, showing the three options parents have for interacting with their children.

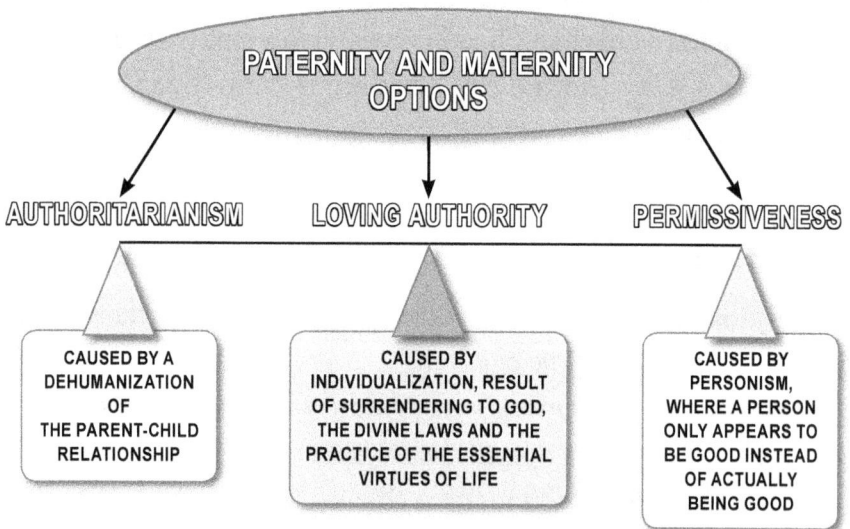

PATERNITY AND MATERNITY OPTIONS

AUTHORITARIANISM

CAUSED BY A DEHUMANIZATION OF THE PARENT-CHILD RELATIONSHIP

LOVING AUTHORITY

CAUSED BY INDIVIDUALIZATION, RESULT OF SURRENDERING TO GOD, THE DIVINE LAWS AND THE PRACTICE OF THE ESSENTIAL VIRTUES OF LIFE

PERMISSIVENESS

CAUSED BY PERSONISM, WHERE A PERSON ONLY APPEARS TO BE GOOD INSTEAD OF ACTUALLY BEING GOOD

Figure 5 – Loving authority, authoritarianism and permissiveness in the parent-child relationship

One of the options is authoritarianism, which was very common in the past. It is caused by the dehumanization of the parent-child relationship.

In authoritarianism the stronger annihilates the weaker. In this model, parents never give their kids any option to decide on their choices for themselves. Instead, they are the ones who always dictate what their children must do.

Nowadays, although these types of relationships, although they still exist they, are far less common. One reason for this is that there are so many Spirits being born in a more evolved state, not so much morally evolved but with an intellectual acuteness that has not been seen before in our planet. These new generations are much more discerning with regard to orders they get from their parents. If this rigidness persists there will be great difficulties in the parent-child relationship itself and kids will have a tendency towards insubordination.

In the past is kids simply "obeyed" their parents without questioning anything. In truth, it wasn't real obedience because obedience is a virtue. Obedience is the behavior of a person who makes an effort to become disciplined. What happened in the past in these authoritative relationships between kids and parents was based on fear. If children dared to contradict their parents, without following their orders, they would give them horrendous beatings. Even if the order was unfair, the children had to follow it.

The authoritarian model does not bring about the transformation of characters. In this relationship, the negative characteristics of the children will be repressed rather than transformed.

For parents, to repress a child's negative characteristics of a child through coercion, making them develop a pseudo-virtues, is not the same thing as helping a child to transform their character through the development of virtues. A true collaboration with God in the development of the child will take place only when their negative characteristics are transformed.

In various societies, especially in countries that are more morally and economically undeveloped, this type of relationship still exists. In our society, generally speaking, it's no longer acceptable, to the point that laws have been created to protect children and teenagers. It's a sign of the evolution of a society that has moved in the direction of the Law of Love. Authoritarianism ends up creating many traumas, resentments and hurtfulness in the parent-child relationship.

For parents who still practice authoritarianism in the family, as in the case of Cindy, there is a great challenge they must face in order to change their ways. But this change should be for the better, not for the worse. What we are seeing nowadays are parents changing from authoritarianism to permissiveness, which is changing from one extreme to another.

Nowadays, it's more common to embrace the other extreme behavior of permissiveness, caused by personalism, where there is tendency toward seeming to be good, as opposed to actually being good. This is because permissiveness is an attempt to run from authoritarianism through the mask of personalism, which engenders *seeming to be* in detriment to actually *being*.

We don't known whether authoritarianism or permissiveness is worse, as both are harmful in different ways. The first hinders education, because children and teenagers obey their parents, not out of love, but from fear of having to endure intense physical and psychological punishments. Nowadays, we even see authoritarianism taking place in reverse, where the dictatorship of the children controls their parents because of permissiveness, in which the figure of a nice father or mother, the super-protectors, gives way to a whole process in which the children are the ones directing the family, as if it this was their natural function.

This is how Andrew behaves. Driven by guilt and the desire to protect his children from their own mother's actions, he behaves in a permissive manner, complicating the lives of the children even more, since they are exposed to both the authoritarianism of the mother and the permissiveness of the father.

Harmony is a loving authority, produced by promoting the individualization of the person, a process that takes place by one's surrendering to God and the Divine Laws, as well as the practice of the essential virtues of life. This is the only true path to a more conscientious paternity and maternity. Few are the parents who behave in this manner, because of all the hard work that it takes to build these harmonious relationships with their children.

In order to become a responsible father and mother, a lot of work is involved. For this reason, the spiritual Mentor Joanna de Ângelis tells us that there are many children who are orphans of living parents. Besides the virtues discussed earlier in this book regarding the conjugal relationship, the parent-child relationship will demand the development of other virtues.

It's only possible to exercise authority in a loving manner when one is an authentic person, following the teaching given by the Master Jesus in Matthew, 5:37: *All you need to say is simply 'Yes' or 'No'; anything beyond this comes from the evil one.*

If the parents have difficulty with a simple 'yes' or 'no', they end up causing great harm. In dealing with the parent-child relationship, these Christian precepts are faithful to a harmony that will free parents from authoritarianism, where everything is 'no', and from permissiveness, where everything is 'yes'. Although merely saying 'yes' or 'no' at the right times seems like a simple thing to do, few are those parents who are capable of exercising this virtue of Christian authenticity.

In the next part we will study how parents can develop this

loving authority, drawing inspiration from *The Spirits' Book* and from *The Gospel According to Spiritism.*

> Question 582. *Can parenthood be considered a mission?*
> "Absolutely. It is a major responsibility that is, certainly, more important to the parents' future than they might suppose. God places a child under the care of parents so that they can help it become a good person. To start with, a child has a fragile and delicate constitution just so that it will assimilate better the good qualities the parents are to nurture in him or her. Unfortunately, some people pay more attention to the trees in their backyards than to their children. They would rather look after their apples and pears than watch over their children's characters. But when a child fails in life as a result of this kind of neglect, the parents are held responsible. The sufferings of that child will fall on them, too – a penalty for not doing what they should have to help the child progress."

> Question 208. *Do the spirits of parents influence the spirit of their child after its birth?*
> "They have a very great influence. As we have already told you, spirits must assist one another's progress. The parents have the mission of developing, through education, the spirits of their children. This is their appointed task, and they can't fail to complete it without experiencing guilt."

The spiritual Mentors' answers tells us that paternity and maternity are more than a mission, they are a *great duty*. This affirmation reminds us of the Law of Duty and the virtue of a conscientious duty, which we have already studied in messages explained by the Spirit Lazarus. Just to refresh our memory, let's recall that duty is the *guardian of our inner rectitude and of our conscience* which warns us at each moment whether we are practicing the Law of Duty and the virtue of duty or not.

Therefore, when someone assumes a commitment with God

to momentarily watch over another immortal Spirit, a brother in humanity who is in the transitory condition of childhood, they assume a consciential duty to collaborate with God, by guiding this child through an education based on good principles. But as this takes a lot of work and, as explained in question 582 of *The Spirits' Book*, parents are often more concerned with taking care of the garden and other superficial matters, than taking care of their own children. This behavior is supported exclusively by the concerns of the ego, as in the example of Andrew and Cindy.

This is the reason why many parents acquire serious conscientious debts, as they disregard the Law of Responsibility. Even though they are free to ignore their previously accepted commitments, they are still responsible for all that they have either done or left undone.

Many, instead of developing a responsible conscience, which is an essential virtue for the development of conscious parenting with authority based on love, tend to develop a guilty conscience, becoming permissive with their children, fulfilling all of their wishes while irresponsibly trying to make up for the real care children need, especially in their first infancy, when their *organization is fragile and delicate*.

> Question 583. *When a child takes the wrong road despite the dedication of good parents, are they still held responsible?*
> "No. As a matter of fact, the more vicious the disposition of the child the greater is the parents' merit for turning the child away from wrong."
> a) If a child, despite neglect and bad examples on the part of the parents, develops in a positive direction, do the parents have any merit for?
> "God is fair."

These two questions above expand on the relation between of the divine justice and parent-child relationships. The mission of parents is guiding their children to the path of goodness, making every effort to form their character. However, they should act as the sower from the evangelical parable, sowing the seeds of love in their hearts, but with the understanding that they are not the ones who will provide the germination of these seeds. That is the responsibility of the children themselves who are also guided through the Divine Laws in their consciences, just like the adults. If, in spite of the good care of the parents, they deviate from the narrow path, the parents will not be responsible for their bad choices. On the other hand, parents also do not have any merit when their kids turn out to be good people after having been brought up with bad examples from their parents.

How can one evaluate if parents have done all that they could for the good of their children? In other words, how can it be known that they accomplished goodness to the best of their abilities? This knowledge can only be found in their own consciences where, as the tribunal of the conscience is incorruptible, that which is just will always prevail.

Now let's study the teaching of St. Augustine, extracted from item 9, chapter XIV of *The Gospel According to Spiritism*:

[...]

Spiritists, realize the importance of humankind. You must recognize that when a body is created, the soul that incarnates in it has come from spirit world with only one purpose: spiritual advancement. Make this clear to yourselves, accept your responsibility, and use all your love to bring this soul nearer to God. This is the mission with which you have been entrusted and for which you will receive a just reward if you fulfill it well. The care and education you give to this child will help in its improvement and future well-being. Remember that God will ask every mother and father, "What have you done with the child who was entrusted to you?" If the child went astray because of something you did or failed to do, your greatest punishment will be to see it suffer among other rebellious spirits, knowing that its future happiness rested at one time in your hands. Then, feeling pangs of guilt, you will ask for a way of redeeming your failings. You will ask for another incarnation for both of you, when you will strive to surround the spirit of that child with the type of loving care that truly enlightens the soul. In the end, it is you who will be surrounded by love, love that emanates from a truly grateful soul.

Don't give up on a child who rejects a parent, or treats a parent with ingratitude. It is not by chance that the child is this way, nor is it an accident that the child is under your care. Such reactions often reveal a dim intuition of the past, from which fact we can conclude that one or the other – the parent or the child – may have hated or harmed the other in the past. In fact, the current life may offer a great opportunity for forgiveness or for redress. Parents, embrace the child who vexes you and say to yourself, "One of us is guilty!" Make yourselves worthy of the supreme joys of parenting by teaching your children that they are on earth in order to perfect themselves, to love, and to make their lives a blessing to others. Be aware, however, that there are many parents who, instead of educating their children to counter those inborn tendencies carried over from their previous lives, actually encourage these tendencies through their feebleness of character or lack of care. Later on, they will have their hearts torn apart by the ungratefulness of their children, and that in itself will start their purification, even in this life.

Still, parenting isn't a task as hard as it might seem. It doesn't require the wisdom of the world. Everyone, whether uneducated or highly learned, can carry out this duty. The Spiritist Doctrine has come primarily to help by illuminating the causes of the imperfections in the human soul.

The good and bad tendencies a child reveals early on have roots in previous lives. This finding is, of itself, deserving of serious study. Clearly, the root of all bad tendencies can be found in selfishness and pride. So be on the lookout for the least sign that will reveal the existence of these tendencies, and attack them before they take deeper root in the child. Do as the good gardener does: Cut off all the defective shoots as soon as they appear on the tree. If you allow selfishness and pride to develop, you shouldn't be surprised, later on, when you are rewarded by ungratefulness.

Where parents have done everything possible for the moral progress of their children, even if unsuccessfully, they have nothing to reproach themselves for and their consciences can rest easy. For the pain that naturally results from the fruitlessness of their efforts, God has in store a great, an immense, consolation: the assurance that this interlude is really only a short delay. They will be able to finish the work they've already begun in another lifetime, and one day their ungrateful children will reward them with love.

The teachings of Saint Augustine deepen that which we have already seen in *The Spirits' Book* and invite us to the practice of several virtues. The great commitment of parents is to bring children closer to God. So that parents can accomplish this task, they must first bring themselves closer to God.

As we have previously reflected upon, their children are immortal Spirits who they have received in a process of co-creation and in collaboration with God, guiding these children of God and our brothers in humanity, to be good persons. This is a task that they will answer for, in every aspect regarding the children, for as long as they, the parents, are responsible for them.

Because Andrew and Cindy are always fighting, they do not have the ability to create the intimate environment that is necessary to form this connection with God and, as a result, their family becomes extremely dysfunctional. This causes them to incur serious debts before their own consciences. If they cannot bring resolution to their troublesome relationship, they will not able to have a good parent-child relationship.

It's essential that the couple assumes the true responsibility of forming a family. Cindy, especially, should reflect upon her function as a mother who feels like a nanny to her own children. This is clearly an indication that she is denying her true role as a mother, which was the role she directly assumed before God when she gave birth to them. Andrew should free himself from the personalism that has led him to assume the role of a super protector. Instead of being only the provider of their material needs, he should also assume the paternal posture of a father who is present in the life of his children.

As St. Augustin says, the task is not so difficult, but it is laborious, as it requires from the parents a constant observation of their own acts and the acts of the children, correcting the children and conducting them to the practice of doing what is good, as they attempt to correct themselves, learning from their own mistakes, Parents must understand that by not making efforts in this direction, they will have to answer for all the harm visited upon the children who were entrusted to them.

Now let's reflect on a detail of the story of Andrew and his family. It relates to the matter of him working too much so that he can provide, according to his beliefs, all that he can for his children.

We will now study what *The Spirits' Books* says about this:

Question 715. *How can we know the limits of our needs?"*
"The sensible person knows them through intuition. There are many others who learn them only by hard experience."

Question 716. *Can't we say that the limits of human needs are established by our bodily structure?*
"Yes, but human beings are insatiable. Nature has set your proper limits, as you rightly observe, by giving you a particular kind of body. But your vices change your constitution and create artificial needs for you."

Question 704. *When humans were given the will to live, did God also provide us with the means of survival?*
"Yes, and if you do not find such means, it is because you lack initiative. God wouldn't instill the will to live in you without furnishing you with the means to survive. This is why Earth has been engineered to produce whatever its inhabitants require."

Many parents make their children orphans of live parents because they invert the values and act as Andrew, making an effort to work excessively to provide that which is superfluous for himself and for his family, forgetting to establish a criteria of what is truly necessary for life.

Although he is a Spiritist, Andrew acts as a spiritualist-materialist, because he withholds from his children that which is most important, his presence in their education, the care and the teachings that are necessary so that they can form their own character, because he is far too occupied with material things.

He could work a little less and provide less of the superfluous, as explained by the spiritual Mentors of Humanity: *their vices alter their constitution and create artificial needs.*

The posture many parents assume, is centered exclusively on materialistic matters, coming from the many vices of the materialistic and hedonist society we live in. This posture creates needs that are not real, in detriment of spiritual matters, which are in truth the real necessity for the immortal Spirits who are momentarily incarnated as their children.

SELF–REFLECTIVE EVALUATION

- Close your eyes and connect with your inner self, exploring the content studied in this meeting.

- Analyze yourself with authenticity, avoiding self-deceit.

- From the content studied, what did you understanding that applies in your life?

- Did the content studied change the way in which you feel the Divine Laws in yourself? If so, what changes did you notice?

- In this meeting, we reflected on the parent-child relationship and the role that it has in the spiritual formation of children. Connect with your inner self, making an effort to feel your relationships with your children, if you have children. For those who do not, reflect upon the meaning of fulfilling the Divine Laws and developing virtues in your other family relationships.

- Now strive to feel in yourself the Law of Duty and the virtue of duty. How do you feel? Reflecting from a more profound understanding of the meaning of the Divine Laws in the family relationships and in the development of the essential virtues, such as the practice of these Laws, has there been an amplification of your will to develop these virtues? What is this like for you?

- How do you feel about your life in applying the content studied? Do you feel that it could improve your life in the search for self-transformation and improve the quality of your activities in the practice of good deeds?

- Now, recognize yourself as the immortal Spirit you are, who brings within the divine purview the determination to evolve until reaching relative perfection, through the pure understanding of the fulfilment of the Divine Laws, through the practice of virtues and by striving to be one with God. Submerge yourself profoundly into this spiritual truth. Feel and see yourself fulfilling the Divine Laws and developing all the essential virtues of Life throughout time, feeling the loving presence of God in your life.

- Gradually, start retuning to a state of alertness. Open your eyes and write down your reflections.

12th Meeting

The Divine Laws and family relationships

part V

Objective – To reflect on the meaning of the Divine Laws in our lives, in order to love, respect and apply them within the family realm.

Initial reflection – *Meditating on the meaning of the Divine Laws in our family relationships.*

- Close your eyes and connect with your inner self, in search of feeling as an immortal Spirit, a child of God, created to evolve and achieve plenitude.

- How do you feel?

- Have you surrendered yourself fully to God and His Laws?

- How have you been dealing with the Divine Laws in your family relationships? Have you been applying them?
- Let your thoughts and feelings flow, avoiding all masks, and avoiding any process of self-deceit. Be true to yourself, analyzing yourself with authenticity.
- Now open your eyes, returning to a state of awareness. Write down your experience: the feelings that you had, the thoughts that came to mind, and the sensations from which you benefited.

REFLECTIONS BASED ON SPIRITISM
QUESTIONS FOR SELF-REFLECTION

- Knowing that the Divine Laws are present in our conscience and that they exist so that we can reach pure and eternal happiness, what actions can we accomplish to love and fulfill them in parent-child relationship?
- What is a practical means that we can use to manifest the divine attributes and develop the essential virtues of Life in the parent-child relationships?

In this meeting we will continue to study the application of the Divine Laws in family relationships, specifically in relation between parents and children.

The Divine Laws and the parent-child Relationships
part II

In this meeting we will continue to work on the story of the family of Andrew and Cindy, focusing on their relationship with their three children. Before we continue, we suggest that you read the complete story transcribed in the previous chapter.

Initially, we will focus on the objective of infancy and the function of parents in the education of their children in this important phase of the new reincarnation of these immortal Spirits.

Let's see what is said in *The Spirits' Book*:

Question 379. *Is the spirit who animates the body of a child as advanced as the spirit of an adult?*
"It may be more so if, before the reincarnation, it had progressed farther than the adult. Actually, only the underdevelopment of the child's organs prevents the spirit from fully manifesting its qualities."

Question 380. *Does a spirit think as a child or as an adult during infancy?*
"Because the brain is underdeveloped during infancy, the spirit cannot show the reasoning capacity of an adult. Its intellectual range, consequently, remains narrow until the infant grows older and its reason evolves. Furthermore, the perturbation the spirit experiences during the process of incarnation does not immediately stop at birth; it ends only gradually, as the body's organs mature."

Question 382. *During childhood, does the incarnate spirit suffer from the constraints its underdeveloped body imposes on it?*
"No, childhood is a necessary stage, a part of the plan of Providence. It is a time of rest for the spirit."

Question 383. *Why must a spirit go through infancy?*
"The purpose of incarnation is to improve the spirit. A spirit is more impressionable during childhood, when the impressions it receives more easily mold its personality, and therefore, promote its progress. To that end, everyone entrusted with the education of a child should contribute."

Question 385. *Why does the character of young people change, especially as they go through adolescence? Is it the spirit that changes?*
"The spirit, as it regains self-awareness reveals itself as it was before incarnation. You have no ideas of the secrets hidden under

the seeming innocence of children. You do not know what they are, what they have been, or what they will be. Still, you love and cherish them as part of yourselves – indeed, to such a degree that the love of a mother for her children is said to be the greatest love one being can have for another. Why do even strangers feel affection and goodwill toward a child? Do you know the origin of that feeling? No? Then we will explain it. Children are beings God sends into new lives. God gives them all the external appearance of innocence, so that even misdeeds of the worst possible nature are concealed in the unconscious memory. The apparent innocence does not mean, then, superiority. Innocence is merely the image of what they ought to be. If they are not, the responsibility is theirs alone.

"But it is not only for themselves that God gives the appearance of innocence to children. It is also for the sake of their parents, whose love is so necessary to them in their fragility. This love would greatly diminish if parents believed their children were harsh or angry by nature. Viewing them as good and gentle, however, they give them all their affection, and surround them with the most minute and delicate care. But when, after fifteen or twenty years, children no longer need this protection and assistance, their real characters begin to emerge. The person who is really good remains good, though even then his or her character reveals many traits and nuances that were hidden earlier. You see that God's ways are always for the best; and for the pure of heart, they are easily explained. But understand this well: the spirit of a newborn may have come from a place where it has acquired habits totally different from yours. How would it be possible for this new being – with feelings, inclinations, and tastes entirely opposed to yours – to adjust to your sphere of life if it did not pass through the sieve of infancy, as Providence has determined? Through the sifting process of infancy, the diversity of spirits who people the universe develops common and harmonious ways of self-expression in the worlds they are called to inhabit. You, too, on dying, may find yourself in a sort of infancy, in the midst of a new community. In your new non-earthly existence you will be unaware of the habits, manners, and relations of a realm that is new to you, and you will find it difficult to express yourself in a language you are not used to – a language livelier than your thought is today."

"There is still another purpose in childhood. Spirits only enter incarnate life in order to improve, to grow. The tender nature of the young makes them more pliable, more open to the advice of individuals whose experience can aid their progress. In this way tendencies toward wrong-doing are re-directed and faulty characters are gradually reformed. God entrusts this moral modeling to the parents as a duty, as a sacred mission of which they will have to give a solemn account. So you see that childhood is not only useful, necessary, indispensable, but that it is the natural result of the laws of God."

Question 844. *Do we have free will from birth?*
"You have it from the moment you develop the will to act. In infancy and early childhood, free will is almost non-existent. It develops and changes its objectives with the development of the faculties. The child applies its free will to the things associated with its age."

Childhood is a very important period for the incarnated Spirit, because it constitutes a phase of rest, in which the Spirit can become more susceptible to education that will form its character. Its free will is restricted so that parents can guide the Spirit adequately towards goodness.

In the education of the children, parents will be engaged with three main functions:

Collaborative – motherhood and fatherhood are very serious commitments, and it's not enough to just co-create, enabling the reincarnation of the immortal Spirit. It's necessarily something more than that. Fathers and mothers are those who assume the commitment of being collaborators with God, in the formation of the character of the brother or sister in humanity who will temporarily be their child.

When parents have the full understanding of their responsibility as collaborators, instead of thinking they are going to live their lives through their children, the educational mission they are accepting can be accomplished much more easily.

Conversely, when parents carry the feeling of pseudo-omnipotence, as Andrew does, they feel responsible for the future choices their children make in life. It's important to emphasize that they are not responsible for future choices their kids will make, which is a conclusion we arrived at in the previous chapter. They are only responsible for their own efforts in the formation of the character of their children in the present existence, during the period in which these immortal Spirits, brothers and sisters in humanity will be under the guidance of the parents. This is the essence of the collaborative function of fatherhood and motherhood.

Directive – the one in which the father and the mother will guide their children towards the practice of doing good, teaching them to love themselves, others and God.

The directive function is essential in the collaboration process with God. It's clear that in order for parents to practice this function with their children, they'll need to practice it with themselves first, otherwise it will be impossible for a father or a mother to serve as guides to their children, teaching them what is good, and strengthening their love without having the knowledge within themselves of what they wish to teach.

It's essential to practice the teachings to be directed to their children, but that does not mean that parents should be perfect. What they should do is to always make efforts to perfect themselves and the only action that can direct one towards perfecting themselves is the practice of love. This constant practice allows parents to safely acquire the conditions that will enable them to guide their children towards these same values, collaborating with God, especially during their infancy.

Guidance – parents are the main guides when it comes to the formation of the character of their children; as they observe the individual characteristics of each child, they reinforce the positive and correct the negative, as is taught in *The Spirits' Book* and in *The Gospel According to Spiritism*, studied in the previous chapter.

The success of this guiding function of forming characters will depend on the relationship parents have with their children. Success can only be achieved when parents are present in the formation of their children, so they can actually notice negative and positive traits, helping kids to transform the first while reinforcing the later.

It's important for parents to avoid the pretension that they are creating the character of the child, realizing, instead, that they are only collaborators in that process, because the Spirit that is momentarily re-incarnated as a child is an immortal Spirit with a millenary baggage, bringing a wholly formed character that has already been developed in other existences. Since they are still in an evolutionary process, their present individualities are still in need of development and are, especially in phases of infancy, very responsive to the reception of proper information that will enable them to change their characters.

This is the objective of spirits reincarnated as children, because in every existence we are re-born to reform our character, reinforcing positive aspects in ourselves, and transforming negative situations.

Suggestive – in this function, parents suggest to their sons and daughters who are now adults, to continue to base their actions in the practice of goodness, reinforcing the teachings given during phases of infancy and adolescence.

It's not up to parents whose kids have grown, especially when they are emancipated, to guide and orientate them directly in their adult lives. During this adult phase, the orientation phase has already passed.

Because so many come from a family culture that is very intrusive, it's common for parents to want to continue to behave as guides in the lives of their adult sons and daughters as if they were five-year-old children. Many parents even keep on referring to their offspring as children throughout their entire lives. Parents must be more aware of this tendency to see their offspring as forever children. If they choose to behave in this way, they will give up their suggestive function and begin to practice **imposition**, creating difficulty in the relationship. They will be imposing their views into the lives of their sons and daughters, as if they were creators and proprietary owners of their adult children, and not the co-creators and collaborators that they are in reality.

It's not up the parents to direct the lives of their adult children. They can and should suggest changes when they perceive any difficulties their sons and daughters may be facing. This is all based on the notion of being collaborators with God.

Therefore, in the adult phase only suggestions are appropriate, as a light form of guidance. They can suggest possibilities of accomplishments, and their sons and daughters will either accept to follow or not, according to their own choices.

This function will vary in accordance with the phases of formation of the child: First infancy from 0 to 7 years of age; second infancy from 7 to 12 years; next is the teenage phase from 12 to 18 years; and lastly, adult, life.

These phases are only general references. They are not set in stone, as they can vary in accordance to the evolutionary level of each incarnated Spirit. Often times we see, for example, children of 6 years of age already in the second infancy, others of the age of 10 already in the teenage phase, and individuals aged 21 or older still acting like teenagers.

The collaborative function exists in all these phases because the greater commitment parents have is to collaborate with God in the formation of their brothers and sisters in humanity who will momentarily be their child. Each one works on their own process of evolution and collaborates with others in their evolution.

This function is so significant that often times we see it being exercised in mediumistic meetings, when Spirits who were mothers and fathers in a certain existence, find their previous offspring in difficult situations in the spiritual world and begin to actively work to help their loved ones rehabilitate and find spiritual health. Often times they do this work during hundreds and even thousands of years, for as long as is necessary in order to help their brothers and sisters in humanity who once where their children.

During infancy, the function of parenting is eminently **directive**, because the child has in this phase a difficulty in practicing abstract thinking. The child in the first stage of infancy thinks in a concrete manner, being incapable of establishing abstract concepts and making rational conclusions about how these concepts can fit into their lives.

Because of the child's incapacity to deal with abstract concepts, their freewill is very limited. This is the reason why they have need of parents to direct their freedom, "trimming their wings" as necessary, in order to direct them to the practice of what is good.

In early childhood, the directive function remains, but the guidance function can already be added to it. In this phase of spiritual and psycho-emotional development of the child, the collaboration will be **directive-guiding**, because the child still needs to be guided since it does not have a great capacity for abstraction, but can already be taught basic concepts that are the building blocks of more abstract concepts.

Around this phase her participation in school becomes more effective. It differentiates from the kindergarten years in which the objective was learning to socialize with others. Now they begin to have contact with more abstract concepts.

Therefore, the child can already be educated in concepts to be reflected upon. They are apt to grasp abstract concepts from more or less seven years of age, depending on the maturity of the reincarnated Spirit. It can be a bit more or a little less, but in general around the age of seven, children can already be educated in abstract concepts.

This action is truly a result of the guidance function, since it mainly aims at character formation. Parents need to be attentive to the character of their children so they can help in guiding them in their development. If they observe negative characteristics in their children, work needs to be done in those areas. Such negativities, for example, may be shown by tendencies toward sexual addiction, violence, dishonesty and others. In that case, children will need a very well-founded guidance so these difficulties don't gain even more traction in their lives.

From middle childhood and on, the child should be encouraged through dialogue to make adequate use of their free will. It's through free will that the child will develop the essential virtues for spiritual growth, such as self-esteem, self-acceptance, self-confidence, self-value, self-respect and self-responsibility.

If the child has a difficulty such as misleading or lying to people, for example, the guidance process needs to be directed towards the realm of honesty and the healthy habits of telling the truth. When parents take the time to observe their children they work towards directing them to return to that which is best for them, for what is good and spiritually sound, envisioning the formation of their character by concentrating on developing their self-love and love towards others.

During adolescence, the function will be guidance-directive, **educating with direction**. While during middle childhood it's more of a directing with guidance, and in adolescence the capacity of abstraction is greater, and thus making guidance more important, but an guidance that is always directed, because the directive function will only end in adult life.

Adolescents already have a greater capacity for abstraction, and elaboration of concepts, that allows parents to find out what their kids think about a certain subject, and have more meaningful dialogues.

The dialogue is a guidance process par excellence that starts at the end of the first infancy and amplifies more and more with each passing year in early childhood, until it reaches its peak in the parent-child relationship during adolescence.

Adolescence is characterized by a great capacity for dialogue, where youngsters can share their thoughts. This capacity for dialogue should be encouraged from infancy, or it may become very difficult to be develop it in adolescence. Parents should make the most of these dialogues in order to guide their children, thus providing an opportunity for difficulties to be transformed.

In adolescence, our children's characters that they developed in past lives will become more evident, especially the negative traits of their characters. Therefore, more guidance is needed in this phase; more ability, effectiveness and affection will be needed in order to direct them towards what is good, and lay the groundwork for the formation of character in the teenager.

Lastly, there's the **suggestive** function, which is the only method that should be used for sons and daughters who have grown to adulthood. For them, the only suitable option would be for parents to give them suggestions in regards to any possible life changes, because they have or at least should have already received the guidance that would have directed the formation of the basis of their character as they were growing up.

Many parents do not put the effort into doing the work of forming their children's character as they grow up, and then, inopportunely, want to do that after they become adults. In that adult phase it's no longer possible to properly exercise the parenting functions of **direction and guidance**. However, knowing that the collaborative function will never end, it's possible for a reeducation based on the suggestive function, which will only happen with the consent of the adult offspring, because this is more a process of reeducation than something that the parents can actually do. When parents want to educate, guiding and directing the children who have become adults, they end up creating many difficulties in their relationships with their adult sons and daughters.

We conclude our studies about the Divine Laws and the family dynamic by taking a look at a parable of the Gospel, The Parable of the Sower, and reflecting upon it within the family context.

Family relationships are an invitation for the sowing of love. To reflect upon the Parable of the Sower is an important exercise, especially for parents, but also for their children and spouses in general. No matter what position we occupy in a family, it's essential for us to see ourselves as sowers of love.

We will study the parable noted by Matthew, 13:3 to 9:

Then he told them many things in parables, saying:
"A farmer went out to sow his seed. As he was scattering the seed, some fell along the path, and the birds came and

ate it up. Some fell on rocky places, where it did not have much soil. It sprang up quickly, because the soil was shallow. But when the sun came up, the plants were scorched, and they withered because they had no root. Other seed fell among thorns, which grew up and choked the plants. Still other seed fell on good soil, where it produced a crop—a hundred, sixty or thirty times what was sown. He who has ears, let him hear."

If we only superficially observe the parable, we might come to the conclusion that this sower is very careless, since he sows all along the path, including in unproductive soil made up of rocks and thorns. In the first place, one could argue that he should only plant on good soil. Why then, did Jesus go to the trouble of making such description, which showed that the sower was sowing without any concern as to where the seeds would fall?

To understand the reason why Jesus presents the sower in this manner, it's necessary to analyze the parable through the lens of a profound psychological understanding, making use of a transpersonal-conscientious analysis. Jesus makes an effort to call our attention not to the sower himself, but to the type of soil that the seeds fall upon.

The function of each member of the family is to **collaborate** with one another so that love is learned by all as brothers and sisters. In this function we are invited to act as sowers of love, regardless of how the other members of the family will receive the seed. Our role is that of a sower of the seeds of love, motivating each person in our family to do the same, in accordance with their capabilities.

That is why it's not up to us as sowers to expect the germination and fruitfulness of the seed. The germination will depend on the soil upon which where it falls, that is to say, the potential of each member of the family.

The choosing of the seeds we are going to plant is our responsibility. We have the seeds of love, renunciation, compassion, meekness, humbleness, tolerance, and solidarity, with constant work in the field of goodness, to create favorable conditions for the health of the family. What each member of the family will do with these seeds is up to them. We must also keep in mind that according to a systemic-transpersonal view, these seeds of love are indestructible and one day will invite others to also become sowers of love.

In the parable, the Master Jesus concentrates his attention more on the soil than on the sower. The different types of soils can be symbolized in the family as six different psychological profiles: along the path, on rocky soils, thorny soil and, yet three other profiles in the good soil, producing each 30, 60 and 100 times the original number of seeds.

In various families, there are people who behave as if they were *along the path*. They remain in the periphery of life, living in a superfluous manner, without real commitment towards their own existence. They are very distant from the freeing Truth, living like robots, distant from the real meaning of life.

The metaphor is an illustration of people who are still living superficially, neither being good nor evil. The seed falls but does not have the means of germinating at that moment.

Others behave as the *rocky soil*, with little soil, where the seed grows quickly and suddenly dies burned by the sun. In this profile are those family members who initially become very motivated with the possibility of evolving and soon after lose their motivation. They recognize the Truth, and are able to envision and awaken to all that is good, right and beautiful, but still do not want to compromise themselves in doing the work needed to live the Truth.

Then there are people who behave like the *thorny soil*. As much as the loving seeds fall on them, these individuals receive

them with the rebelliousness of an unloving and deliberately suf-
focate them because of the ascendancy of egoic emotions like pride,
selfishness, vanity, and presumption. They still insist on living as if
life is not a divine blessing for their own evolution, delaying the
search for the real meaning of their existence.

Fortunately, there are those who are like the *good soil*, who
look for a meaning to their own lives, seeing it as a divine blessing
for their evolution. They reach out for the Truth that frees with the
objective of mixing the soil, so that it can produce in accordance
with its fertility.

Some will produce *thirty times*, that is, they initiated the process of fertilization of their own existence. They have gone through
stages in other profiles and thanks to the pain they have experienced, they have decided to accept divine love and begin the pro-
duction of love within themselves. Life, for them, starts to have a
true meaning – to love.

Others produce *seventy times*, symbolizing those who are already in an improved situation. They have been awakened for a
longer time and use the truth to transform their lives for the better.
They are able to detect the true meaning of life and make an effort
to live it with quality.

Others produce a *hundred, times* since they are already faithful to the Truth. Their lives are filled with meaning, and are also
filled with abundance of excellent quality. They utilize all of their
resources to live as the eternal Beings that they truly are, in a pure
communion with God.

In the context of the family, we create a great difficulty by
wanting all members of our family to be in the profile of the *good
soil*, preferably producing a *hundred times*.

Could this be possible on a planet of trials and atonements?
No! That would only take place in more spiritually evolved worlds.

We ask: if, for example, a partner has the profile of the *thorny soil*, as in the case of Cindy, how would this marriage be?

If we have a child who fits the *along the path* profile – the superficial one, who does not care about anything, and is not willing to become more spiritual, how will their educational process proceed?

If we have a father or a mother fitting the profile of the *rocky soil*, what will the day to day life with them be like?

Lastly, if we have anyone in our family, who fits in any of the inferior profiles, what should we do with those relationships?

If we accept this momentary situation of living with a spouse who fits the profile of the *thorny soil*, a child in the *along the path* profile, a father, a mother, or a sibling in the *rocky soil* profile, and we do not want to falsely transform them into *good soil*, we will have a challenging experience in our marriage, in our parent-child relationship, and in all other relationships. However, we can overcome these challenges and live in relative harmony, if we act as the sowers of love.

Given the way Jesus describes the sower who went out to sow, would it be reasonable to assume that he is a farmer? No, a farmer would not sow sporadically, and he would not sow the seeds *along the path*, or among the thorns, on the rocky places, but only on the good soil.

The sower Jesus is referring to is different. Symbolically, it's a sower of seeds of love, not a reaper.

Likewise, the day to day living of family life will be a seeding of love. Each family member will contribute with the seeds they have. Obviously, we can only sow if we are already in the position of the *good soil*, producing our own seeds of love, virtues of the immortal Spirit. In the profiles of *the thorny soil, rocky soil* or *along the path*, we still haven't awakened to the possibility of being sowers.

Thus, it is necessary that the first step we must take to become a sower is the fertilization of our own hearts.

Let's suppose we are already sufficiently spiritually developed to fit into the profile of the *good soil*, even if we produce less than 30 times. What is our function within the family? It is to sow the seeds of love. For this type of sower, it does not matter where the seeds fall, because they should be thrown in all types of soil. What matters for the sower is to do his part – to sow!

We know that through the Law of Evolution, all those who are in the *along the path* profile, *rocky soil* and *thorny soil* profiles will eventually attain to the *good soil* profile. Passing through these profiles causes pain and suffering, but we know that this will make it so that they gradually become a fertile soil.

It's then that we find the greatest challenges in family life. We most certainly do not want anyone in our family suffering, especially in the case of parents not wanting their children to undergo any pain or suffering. This feeling is perfectly natural for parents to have, but because of the planet we live on, which is a world of trials and atonements, it would be impossible for anyone's children not to undergo any pain or suffering.

This feeling parents have, in truth is based on a projective mechanism, where parents do not want to suffer with their children.

However, if any of our family members fit into the *along the path*, *rocky soil* or *thorny soil* profiles, pain and suffering are inevitable, as those seemingly bad experiences are part of the mechanism that will move us in the direction of the *good soil* profile.

We can use drug addiction, a very common day to day situation that takes place in many families as an example.

The parents, who are spiritually aware will sow the seeds of love in the hearts of their children, especially through example, giving them guidance about the negative aspects of using drugs.

Here the parents are behaving like collaborators in the formation of their children's character, guiding them to what is good.

If the child already has a tendency to fit into a *good soil* profile, guidance will produce an immediate effect and he or she will surely never have to experience being a drug addict. But what if this child is not in this profile? Is it possible that we have within our family someone who is presently in a profile other than that of the *good soil*?

On a planet of trials and atonements, yes, it will be common for us to have children, brothers, parents and spouses who fit into any of the first three profiles, instead of the last two.

A conscientious father and mother will guide their children regardless of the profile in which they are found to be. As sowers of love they will give directions as many times as necessary, doing their part and collaborating with God in the formation of the character of their children.

If the children however, are in the *along the path, rocky soil* or above all, in the thorny soil profile, the words of guidance their parents offered will not have any immediate effect. They will however, most certainly germinate later on, because the seeds of love are everlasting.

The guidance given by the parents will remain in the mind of the child. Even if the child ends up using drugs, falling deep into addiction, and going through the worst moments of their lives they will remember the parental guidance received. Even if this child dies of an *overdose*, they will remember these teachings after disincarnating. They will remember these teachings after disincarnating. The seeds of love will remain in its psychosphere. The parents can cry over their death, but if they have offered all the guidance they could, they should rest assured that they have done their part in the formation of the character of their child.

We used drug addiction as an example but the same analysis is valid for any type of vice, whether of a physical or moral nature, as we may notice in the character of our children, partner, bother, father or mother etc. We can always play the role of the sower who does not pre-select the soil it has come to plant.

To fulfill the role of the sower well, it's necessary that each one of us can reflect on the following thought: *This son is not mine, this daughter is not mine. It's a child of God, a brother or a sister in humanity, who is with me momentarily so that I can collaborate in the formation of its character, and not to labor on his behalf. The wife/husband is not my creation. This person is with me in a partnership. This earthly father is not mine, he is a brother in humanity, momentarily in the condition of a father.*

The lesson of the Parable of the Sower should always be in our minds, so that we know how to better dedicate ourselves in the functions we are able to perform. If we diverge from this loving understanding, we will engage in a pseudo-omnipotent behavior, thinking, it's my child, my husband, my wife etc., and I am responsible for the choices that they make, and for their spiritual evolution. Could this really be the reality? When not even God takes this position when it comes to us! God created the Laws, and we only follow them from the moment in which we awaken spiritually. God neither does not interfere, nor obligates us; instead, God awaits until we reach maturity.

If we are, at this very moment, being invited to share our experience with a certain brother in humanity, a wife, husband, son, daughter, mother, father etc., we should center ourselves in the real power that is given to us: the power of transforming our lives and serving as an example to our family members, sowing the seeds of love in our home.

By following this mindset, we will disconnect from behaviors such as pseudo-omnipotence, despotism and impotence, while making our own lives easier, being able to say to ourselves: *I am doing my part, offering my best to my son, my daughter, my husband or wife, my brother, my father, my mother etc. Whether they will follow my guidance or not, my suggestions in the direction of what is good, wholesome and admirable, as I have done with my life, is completely up to them.*

In order to act in this way, we are invited to synchronize with the loving power, fruit of the development of our self-conscience, producer of the conscientious duty. This synchronization occurs when we utilize this power to accomplish actions of transformation in our own lives.

It's imperative that we sow, otherwise we will become anxious individuals, placing ourselves in an undesirable and dysfunctional mindset, a place for those who want immediate answers.

Sowing is always an important task for our harmony and the harmony of our family, in which we should sustain with the strength of our values, always guiding.

It's important to remember the part of the Lord's Prayer in which Jesus teaches: *let your will be done.* What is the will of God for all of us? God wills our evolution, so that we may improve and become blissfully happy. This is the will of God, which is identical for all of God's children, and all of God's creation. When will God's will become manifest? When I, as a child of God want it to happen, or at a time when God already knows it will unfold?

God created Laws that will take us to the maximum point. Since these Laws are inevitable, we cannot run away from this path of self-perfecting, of evolution. The Divine Law also allows each one of us the freedom to awaken and follow our path to progress.

This reality will brings us about a real mindset, moving us away from the false mindset of self-deceit. In this new reality we will feel capable of making our family healthier, developing a self-conscious conscience, practicing the duty of conscience, and learning to love ourselves as brothers, because we were created by God with this greater objective. We have a clear certainty of all of this because the energy that we feel when connected to God, stimulates the emotions of love, renunciation, compassion etc., and this energy cannot possibly be cunterfeited. The Divine Providence watches over all of us, so that we can practice the exercises of love, feeling and living it fully.

It's very good to trust in the Divine Providence. One of the most heartwarming and comforting feelings in life, is to trust in a Divine Providence that watches over us and the whole Universe. Those who do not trust in the Divine Providence live as abandoned Beings in the Universe. Without any doubt, it's a very sad and unpleasant way to live.

Those of us who are at this present moment able to fully trust in the Divine Providence can truly feel that this is how things are, that this is not an invention of some kind, because we can feel it in our skin, in our hearts, beating stronger with each passing moment. We feel in the ease and tranquility that take over our lives, not as a blind faith, but from a belief arrived at by deep reflection, by feeling and living the Truth.

This conviction makes it possible to overcome any difficulty so that we can live well in our family, in a healthy and happy manner. As a result, the Universe will open up to us, as we are determined and ready to live Life in a more fulfilling and useful way.

SELF-REFLECTIVE EVALUATION

- Close your eyes and connect with your inner self, exploring the content studied in this meeting.

- Evaluate yourself in an authentic manner, avoiding self-deceit.

- From the content studied, what do you understand that applies in your life?

- Did the content studied change the way in which you feel the Divine Laws in yourself and within the family? If so, what changes were these?

- In this meeting, we reflected on the relationship between the parents and their children and the duty that parents have in the spiritual formation of their children. Connect with your inner self, making an effort to feel in yourself your relationship with your children, if you have them. If not, reflect on the meaning of fulfilling the Divine Laws and developing these virtues in your other family relationships.

- Now, strive to feel in yourself the Law of Duty and virtues of duty. How do you feel? Starting from a more profound understanding of the Divine Laws in the family relationship and from the realization of the need to developing of the essential virtues as the axis of these Laws, has there been an increase in your will to develop these virtues? What is this like for you?

- How do you feel while applying the content studied? Do you feel that it could improve your life in the search for self-transformation and in your efforts to practice good deeds?

- Now, recognize yourself as the immortal Spirit you are, who brings within the divine purview the determination to evolve until reaching relative perfection, through the pure understanding of the fulfilment of the Divine Laws, through the practice of virtues and by striving to be one with God. Submerge yourself profoundly into this spiritual truth. Feel and see yourself fulfilling the Divine Laws and developing all the essential virtues of Life throughout time, feeling the loving presence of God in your life.

- Gradually start returning to a state of alertness. Open your eyes and write down your reflections.

Appendix

How to conduct Groups of Fraternal Coexistence for the Integral Education of the Human Being[14]

The methodology applied in groups meeting to study the Fraternal Coexistence for the Integral Education of The Human Being groups, is centered on the immortal Spirit, as a way to promote its progress into greater levels of evolution.

The most important objective of the group isn't only to study contents in an intellectualized manner, but to live in an atmosphere of harmony and fraternity, in an effort to avoid making

---

14 Authors note: Taken from chapter 6 of the book – *The Spiritist* Center *and the Promotion of the Immortal Spirit* – of our authorship – By Editora Espiritizar

the study group meetings reproduce the same environment experience in regular school meetings.

In the group of fraternal living, Spiritism is studied in a systematic and self-reflective manner, always bringing the content to our day to day lives, as a tool for the promotion of the immortal Spirit. The intention is for all participants to be educated by a self-reflective means in which the exchange of experiences of what they are feeling in regards to the content studied can be applied in their daily lives.

In this fraternal environment, we should share the feelings that emerged from our reflections, so that the components of the group can exercise affection, by building fraternal ties in which with time, will become the norm within the group, as once occurred in the earliest Christian churches. This is the main function of the study of Spiritism.

GUIDE FOR THE FRATERNAL MEETINGS[15]

1st Stage: Individual reflection about the topic (duration 6 to 10 minutes) – the facilitator of the group proposes the theme to be reflected upon, and each participant can briefly meditate upon it, analyzing how they feel in relation to the topic and analyzing the degree to which they are applying the concepts studied in their lives.

2nd Stage: Spiritist reflection (duration 60 minutes) – participants are divided into subgroups, the content proposed is studied (at this stage we can use different group dynamics). In addition to the cognitive study it's important for the facilitator to motivate each participant to meditate over the content, making an effort to

---

15 Author's Note: The time stipulated here is a suggestion. If it is not possible each meeting can be divided in two parts.
'Notas de fim'

reflect on the significance of the teachings, so that they eventually feel them, and then find ways to apply these teachings in their lives.

Each participant is invited to delve into themselves to reflect upon the concepts studied, so that the focus is not only that content, which is merely an incentive; we must emphasize that the main objective is the promotion of the incarnated immortal Spirits, in such a way that they can learn to solve their own problems, loving and fulfilling the Divine Laws present in their consciences.

In order for the objective of this stage to be reached, the facilitator can propose the following question to the group:

- How can the content studied be applied in my life?

- The questions placed at the beginning of each Spiritist reflection should also be used.

3rd Stage: Dialogue about what has been learned (duration of 20 to 30 mins) – with the participants in a circle, in a larger group, the facilitator will encourage the dialogue between the participants about the theme studied and about the practical application in their personal life activities in which they practice good towards others.

It's important that each participant speaks about themselves, of their own thoughts, feelings and their wish to apply what they have learned, avoiding generic conclusions that are purely cognitive and simplistic applications of the content studied, such as: *we should do this or that, we do this, Kardec said that, the spiritual Mentor Andre Luis says this* etc. Such considerations are very impersonal and counterproductive, in light of the proposed objective.

In the reflective study, everyone is invited to speak in the first person. Each one should bring their own reflections, thoughts, feelings and ideas about how they intend to act, motivated by the desire of self-transformation.

For this reason, the greatest foundation of the Groups of Fraternal Living for the Integral Education of the Being is fraternity. By practicing this fraternity, this fellowship, it will be possible to relive practices of the first Christians, who followed the guidance of Jesus: *My disciples will be recognized by their love for one another.*

In this activity, we are invited to open ourselves up fraternally to one another, showing our humanity, our pains, our anxieties. Finally, we are invited to practice that which is seen in chapter 1, starting from the words of the spiritual Mentor Emmanuel, explaining how the original Christian churches of Antioch and Corinth operated: *"They all felt united by supreme fraternal ties; a sense of solidarity was established as a divine basis; the pain and the joys of one belonged to all."*

When we go through these motions as a group, participants grow with the help of one another. Those who have a greater experience serve as a reference for the ones in the lower degrees, and everyone evolves in unison, through the practice of pure fellowship.

4ᵗʰ **Stage: self-reflective evaluation (duration 10 minutes)** – if there is a need; the facilitator will highlight the important points, always maintaining the connection between the content studied and our own lives. After these brief commentaries, the group will be lead to the final self-reflective evaluation, so that in a state of introspection, each component can evaluate what was studied and share with the group their feelings and impressions, and together, the group can plan out how to apply in their daily lives what they have learned.

5ᵗʰ **Stage: Fraternal living** – after the prayer ending the meeting, if suitable, tea can be served so that everyone can socialize in an informal manner.

Bibliography[16]

Kardec, Allan. *The Spirits' Book* – English translation by the Allan Kardec Educational Society (AKES).

Kardec, Allan. *The Gospel According to Spiritism* – English translation by the Allan Kardec Educational Society (AKES).

The Wholly Bible / New International Online Version – www.biblegateway.com

---

16 Author is referring to Brazil – Tr.
Original bibliography refers to the texts in Portuguese of different edition.

www.ingramcontent.com/pod-product-compliance
Lightning Source LLC
Chambersburg PA
CBHW051956090426
42741CB00008B/1416